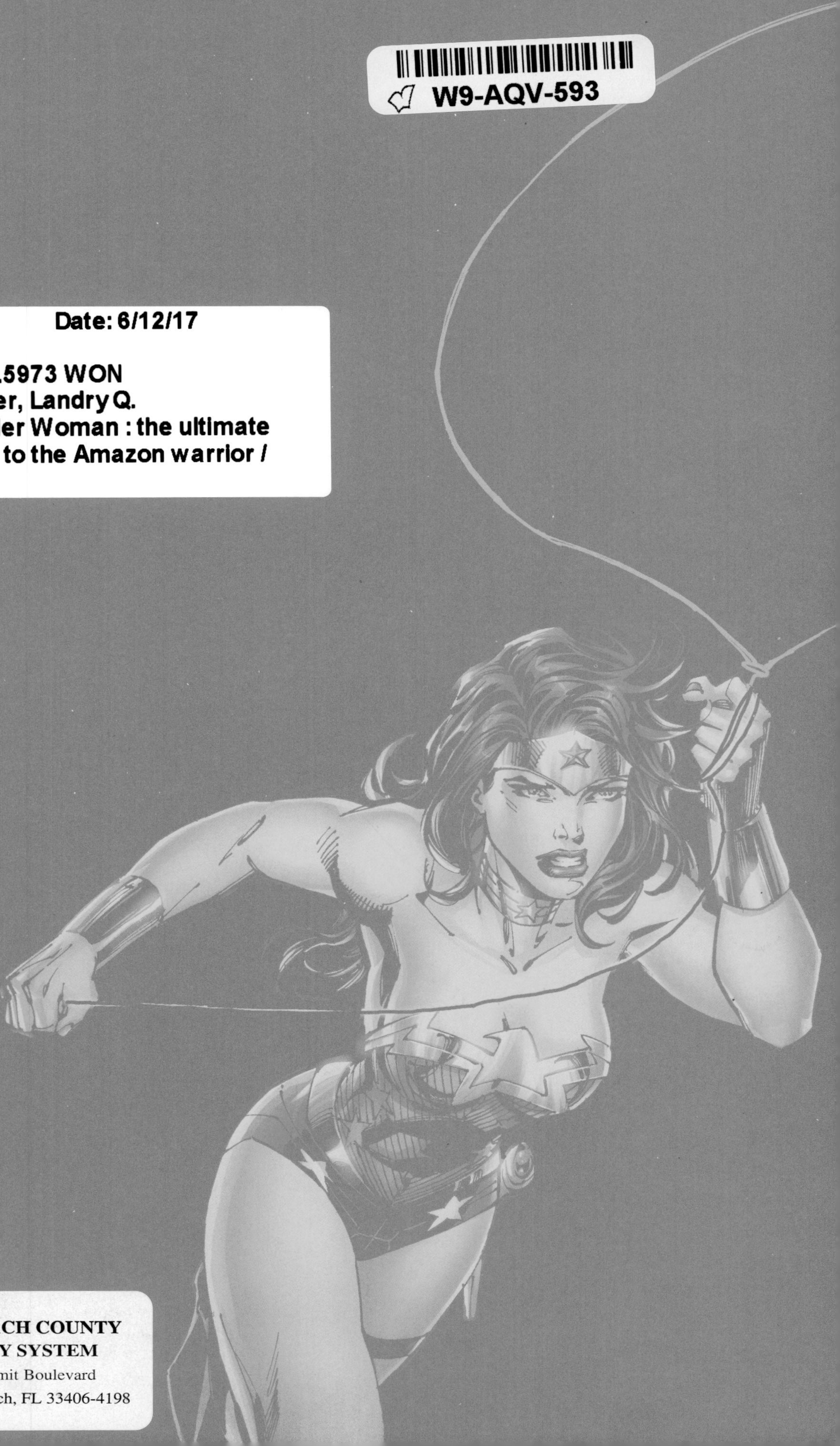

WONDER WOMAN™

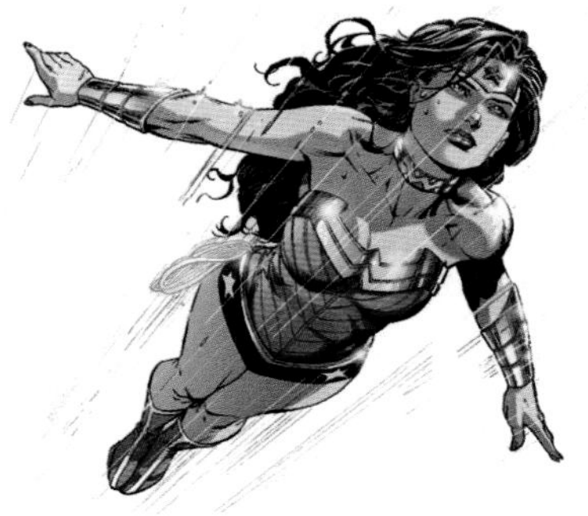

Project Editor Lisa Stock
Editor Kathryn Hill
Senior Designer Clive Savage
Designers Paul Drislane, Ian Midson
Pre-Production Producer Rebecca Fallowfield
Senior Producer Mary Slater
Managing Editor Sadie Smith
Managing Art Editor Ron Stobbart
Publisher Julie Ferris
Art Director Lisa Lanzarini
Publishing Director Simon Beecroft

Designed for DK by Dynamo Limited

First American Edition, 2017
Published in the United States by DK Publishing
345 Hudson Street, New York, New York 10014

17 18 19 20 21 10 9 8 7 6 5 4 3 2 1
001–299070–May/2017

Published in Great Britain by Dorling Kindersley Limited.
A catalog record for this book is available from the Library of Congress.
ISBN: 978-1-4654-6072-1

DK books are available at special discounts when purchased in bulk for
sales promotions, premiums, fundraising, or educational use.
For details, contact: DK Publishing Special Markets, 345 Hudson Street,
New York, New York 10014 SpecialSales@dk.com

Printed and bound in China by Hung Hing

A WORLD OF IDEAS:
SEE ALL THERE IS TO KNOW
www.dk.com

THE ULTIMATE GUIDE
TO THE AMAZON WARRIOR

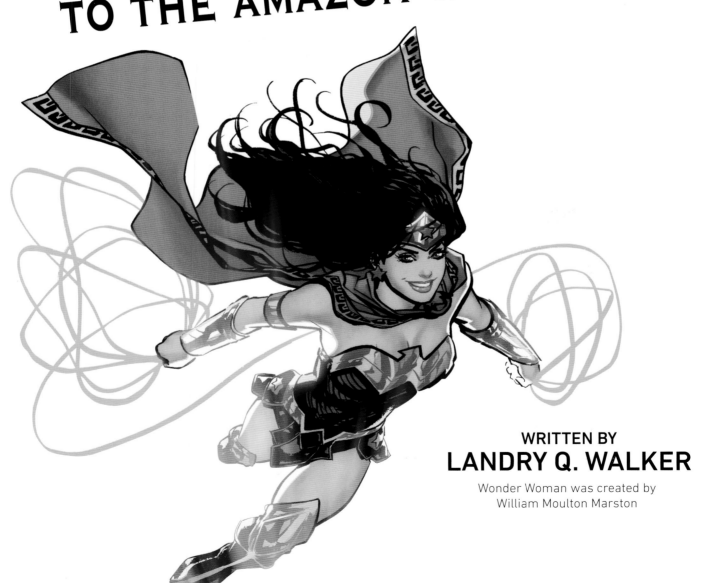

WRITTEN BY
LANDRY Q. WALKER

Wonder Woman was created by
William Moulton Marston

CONTENTS

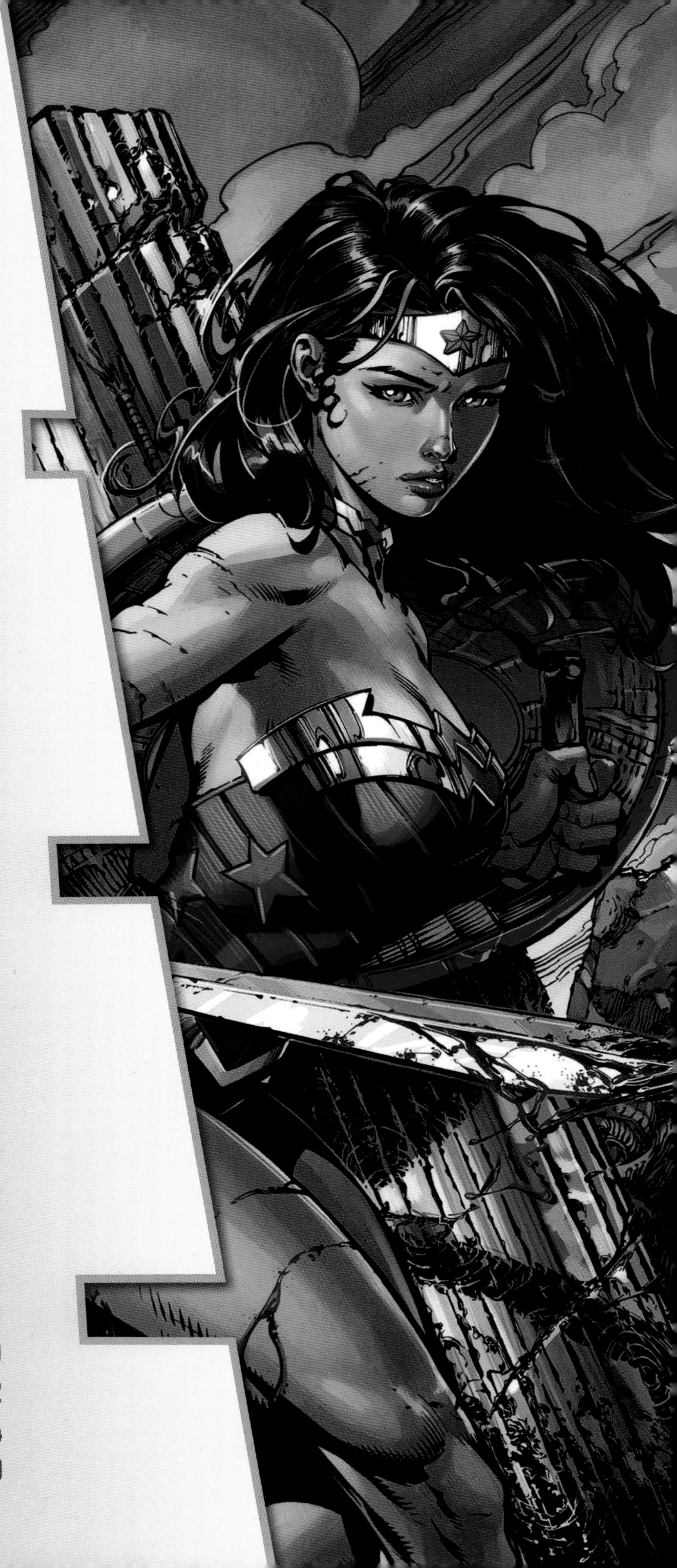

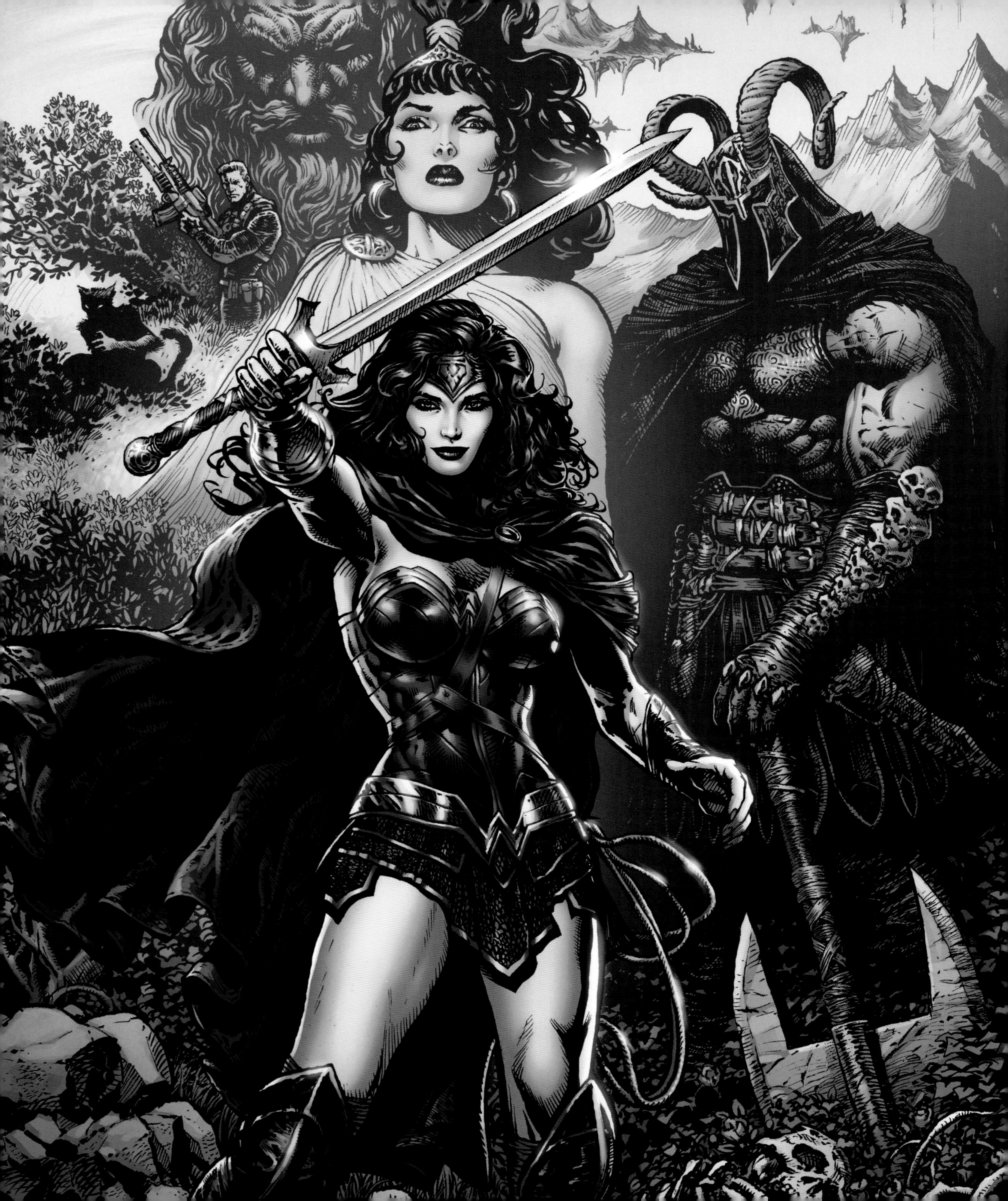

FOREWORD

SHE IS DIANA OF THEMYSCIRA. She is warrior, peacemaker, ambassador, advocate. She is exile and pioneer. She is the stranger in the strange land. She has, alternately (and repeatedly) been goddess and mortal, died, reborn, recreated, and reimagined.

I returned to DC Comics to write Wonder Woman in the spring of 2016, and, things being as they often are in the world of comic book publishing, the deadlines were already looming large and hungry.

Diana—and she's almost always Diana to me, the very nature of who she is inherently inseparable from the name she was given by those first people who had never seen anyone (let alone a woman!) do the things she can do—wouldn't have flinched. I flinched. I stared at the blank screen and the words "Page One" and "Panel One," and flailed. I knew I wanted to start with something iconic, and had settled on "Bullets and Bracelets." They are, after all, Diana's thing. Springsteen does four-hour concerts. Batman leaps out of the darkness and traumatizes criminals. Diana deflects fully automatic weapon fire with her vambraces. That's what she does. It's as much a part of her cultural identity as the tiara and the lasso. For the first time, though, I found myself truly thinking about what it meant that she could do this. In the end, I wrote the following as a preface to my collaborator on the issue, the artist Matthew Clark: *"Just stop and think about this for a second. Think about what it means that she can do this. Diana's reaction time and perception are such that she can intercept and block a bullet—a tiny little bullet!—moving at upwards of 2,400 feet per second. And she can do it to multiple bullets. And she can keep the ricochets from causing collateral damage, from injuring innocents. And we just take that she can do this for granted."*

Which, of course, is precisely my point. We take much of what Diana can do—and more crucially—much of who she is and what she represents, for granted. We see vambraces and thigh-high boots and the solid gold bustier and the Golden Lasso of Truth and we see "just another Super Hero." We think of Lynda Carter, and—if not already, then soon—Gal Gadot. But we don't really think about what it means to be Wonder Woman.

That she exists at all is a literary miracle, all the more so due to her time and place of creation. A character who burst onto the scene at the end of 1941, she embodied feminism and inherently progressive values. Born into a utopia of peace, she leaves of her own accord to enter a world at war, to fight against injustice on every level. Not simply to hand down a spanking—sometimes literally—to the bad guys, but to advocate that there is a better way for us to live. That a world of mutual respect and understanding is far better than one without; that a world of tolerance and equality is worth fighting for.

Her evolution as an advocate for inclusivity and love is the natural by-product of this, something that her creators would have adored. This is, perhaps, the most remarkable thing about her: Where so many other Super Heroes have retained their core intent, to deliver action and thrills, Diana has as well, but with a grander social purpose. If we look to our heroes as icons to emulate, it is Wonder Woman who has most fully embraced that office. She inspires us to be better than we are, not solely to ourselves, but to one another. For this reason, she remains a remarkably challenging character for many to understand. Like us, she changes with time. Like us, her thinking evolves. Like us, her conscience grows. Superman will always be Superman; Batman will always be, in the end, an eight-year-old boy weeping over his parents in a dark alley. But Diana's message—her very heart—grows as we grow.

It's in the name we gave her when she came to our world. She is not simply a woman capable of wondrous feats, nor is she a woman that so many wondered at. She shows us an ideal, and challenges us to reach for it. She asks us to be better than we are. She makes us wonder if we can be—in our hearts, to ourselves, to one another—the people she believes us to be.

She continues to wonder.
We should continue to strive.

Greg Rucka
Portland, Oregon, October 2016

INTRODUCTION

NOT YOUR AVERAGE SUPER HERO, Wonder Woman was created at a time when the majority of Super Heroes were costumed crime-fighters bent on using their fists to solve their problems. Wonder Woman presented the world with something different, something arguably better. She represented a promise of solutions to our societal problems that extended beyond brute force and guns. Wonder Woman would stand for a message from the Greek Gods telling us that *we, humanity, should be better.*

Wonder Woman is the modern-day, unambiguous incarnation of a hero from classic Greek mythology. She is a continuation of stories we have been telling for thousands of years. She was chosen by the Olympian Gods, given a quest to fulfill, and the tools needed to see her mission through. As heroic as Perseus or Odysseus before her, Wonder Woman sacrifices her own immortality, without hesitation, for the greater good of humanity.

One could argue that where Superman gives us authority and Batman offers us vengeance, Wonder Woman teaches us the value of forgiveness, peace, and compassion. Through her actions she demonstrates the importance of equality and the dangers of oppression in all its forms.

Wonder Woman is so much more than a Super Hero who wears a colorful outfit and battles sinister super-villains. She is a powerful symbol that, through her heroic actions, helps us discover our own hidden strengths while bluntly exposing our weaknesses. Through her stories we learn about ourselves, which has always been the purpose of the greatest myths and legends.

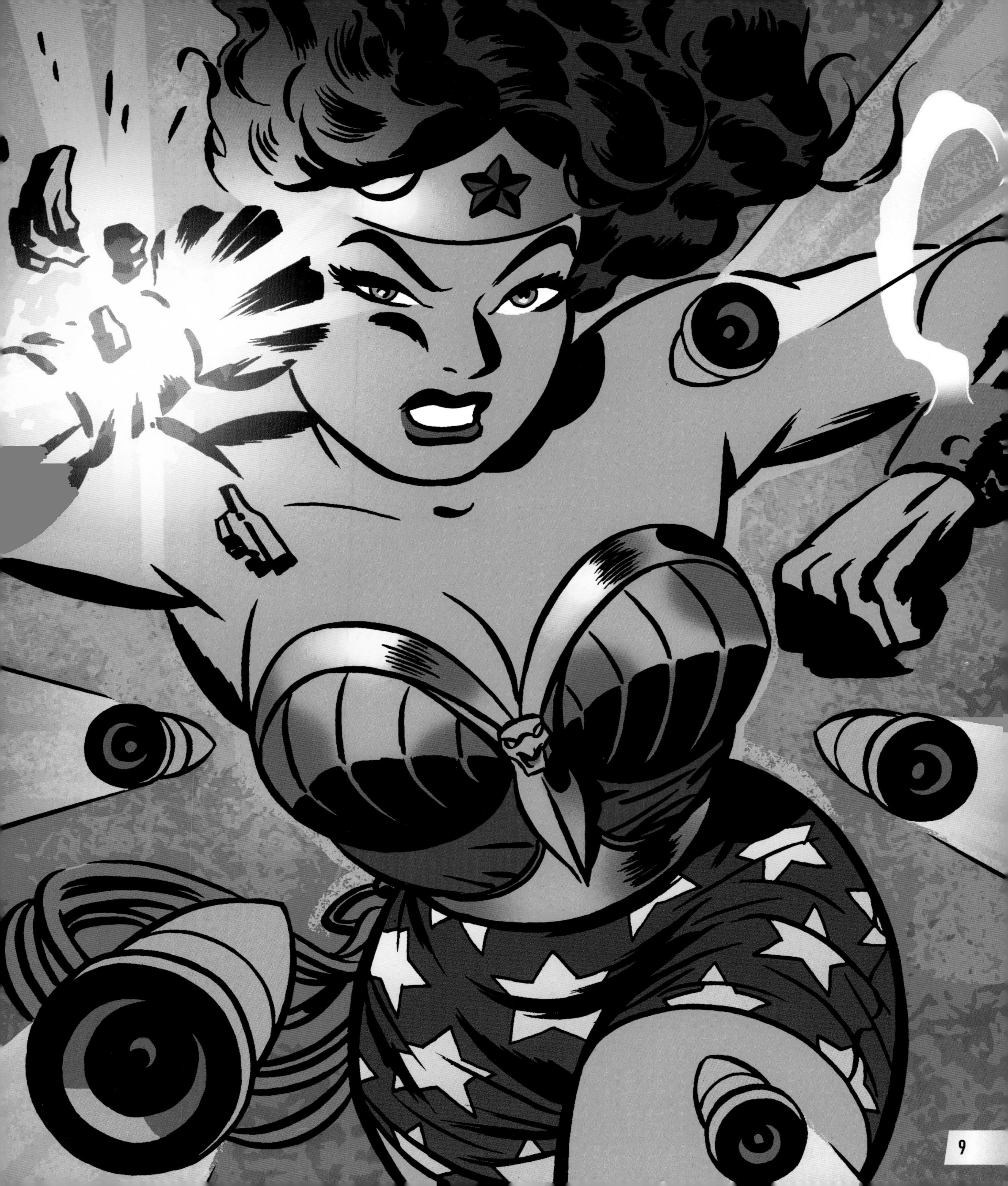

START

Wonder Woman, Princess Diana, leaves Paradise Island with injured pilot Steve Trevor.

Once in America, Wonder Woman encounters young nurse Diana Prince, gaining permanent use of the Prince identity in the process.

Wonder Woman joins the Justice Society of America.

Priscilla Rich succumbs to jealous madness and becomes Cheetah.

Wonder Woman meets Etta Candy and the Holliday Girls, together defeating Doctor Poison and saving Steve.

Wonder Woman battles the Gestapo agent Baroness Paula von Gunther.

Doctor Psycho discovers he can hypnotize people, drawing on their mind power to create illusions.

Wonder Woman leads the Amazons and Valkyries in a battle against the God of War.

The Amazons leave Earth for another dimension to recharge their powers.

Wonder Woman battles the Paper Man.

Donna Troy leaves Paradise Island and joins the Teen Titans as Wonder Girl.

Steve Trevor is killed by Doctor Cyber.

The God of War sends an agent to test Wonder Woman—the Crimson Centipede.

The Justice League and the Justice Society battle Anti-Matter Man.

Wonder Woman almost marries a cruel monster.

With the Amazons gone, Wonder Girl gets an apartment and a new look.

Doctor Cyber's face is destroyed.

Wonder Woman undergoes 12 trials to prove she is ready to rejoin the Justice League.

Wonder Woman meets Cathy Perkins and fights the gang called THEM!

I-Ching is killed by a sniper just as the Amazons return and Wonder Woman regains her lost powers.

THREADS OF FATE

Wonder Woman has had many adventures through the ages. Here are some of the most important events that have shaped the Amazon's career as a Super Hero.

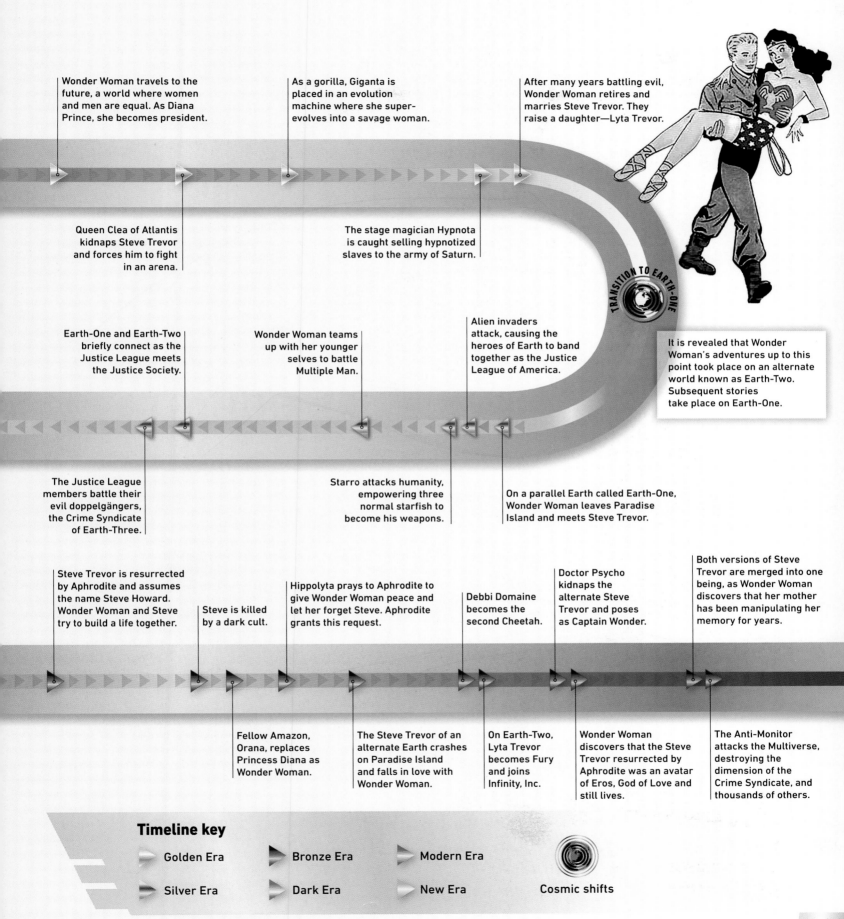

Wonder Woman travels to the future, a world where women and men are equal. As Diana Prince, she becomes president.

As a gorilla, Giganta is placed in an evolution machine where she super-evolves into a savage woman.

After many years battling evil, Wonder Woman retires and marries Steve Trevor. They raise a daughter—Lyta Trevor.

Queen Clea of Atlantis kidnaps Steve Trevor and forces him to fight in an arena.

The stage magician Hypnota is caught selling hypnotized slaves to the army of Saturn.

TRANSITION TO EARTH-ONE

Earth-One and Earth-Two briefly connect as the Justice League meets the Justice Society.

Wonder Woman teams up with her younger selves to battle Multiple Man.

Alien invaders attack, causing the heroes of Earth to band together as the Justice League of America.

It is revealed that Wonder Woman's adventures up to this point took place on an alternate world known as Earth-Two. Subsequent stories take place on Earth-One.

The Justice League members battle their evil doppelgängers, the Crime Syndicate of Earth-Three.

Starro attacks humanity, empowering three normal starfish to become his weapons.

On a parallel Earth called Earth-One, Wonder Woman leaves Paradise Island and meets Steve Trevor.

Both versions of Steve Trevor are merged into one being, as Wonder Woman discovers that her mother has been manipulating her memory for years.

Doctor Psycho kidnaps the alternate Steve Trevor and poses as Captain Wonder.

Steve Trevor is resurrected by Aphrodite and assumes the name Steve Howard. Wonder Woman and Steve try to build a life together.

Hippolyta prays to Aphrodite to give Wonder Woman peace and let her forget Steve. Aphrodite grants this request.

Debbi Domaine becomes the second Cheetah.

Steve is killed by a dark cult.

Fellow Amazon, Orana, replaces Princess Diana as Wonder Woman.

The Steve Trevor of an alternate Earth crashes on Paradise Island and falls in love with Wonder Woman.

On Earth-Two, Lyta Trevor becomes Fury and joins Infinity, Inc.

Wonder Woman discovers that the Steve Trevor resurrected by Aphrodite was an avatar of Eros, God of Love and still lives.

The Anti-Monitor attacks the Multiverse, destroying the dimension of the Crime Syndicate, and thousands of others.

Timeline key

▷ Golden Era ▶ Bronze Era ▷ Modern Era ◉ Cosmic shifts

▷ Silver Era ◀ Dark Era ▷ New Era

11

TIMELINE

Wonder Woman rallies the Amazons to battle against the Anti-Monitor.

The plane of Diana Rockwell Trevor, mother of a young Steve Trevor, is shot down over Themyscira.

Donna Troy's history is cosmically rewritten and she becomes the hero Troia.

Wonder Woman fights the new Cheetah, Barbara Ann Minerva, for the first time.

Wonder Woman's publicist, Myndi Mayer, dies.

During the last battle with the Anti-Monitor, Wonder Woman dies as the Multiverse is collapsed into one reality.

The Multiverse is gone, but a new Earth is created in its wake.

The child of Hippolyta is given life, and named Diana in memory of the mortal pilot Diana, who fought alongside the Amazons.

On the new Earth, Princess Diana is chosen by the Gods to become Wonder Woman, traveling from Themyscira with injured pilot Steve Trevor.

Circe attacks Wonder Woman.

Wonder Woman spends a year as Diana Prince, secret agent.

Wonder Woman rescues Vanessa Kapatelis and seeks medical care for her.

Cassie joins a new version of the Teen Titans.

Vanessa Kapatelis becomes the Silver Swan. Sebastian Ballesteros is made the first male Cheetah by Urzkartaga.

Wonder Woman executes Max Lord.

The Themysciran Embassy is attacked by Medusa.

Checkmate infiltrates the Themysciran Embassy.

Wonder Woman pulls the Earth with her Golden Lasso of Truth.

As Wonder Woman, Princess Diana is chosen to leave Themyscira with the stranded pilot Steve Trevor.

Darkseid attacks Earth. The Justice League forms to battle this threat.

Wonder Woman meets Zola.

Hippolyta turns into a statue when Hera discovers that Wonder Woman is the daughter of Zeus.

The Flash travels back in time and accidentally alters reality, erasing everything and starting existence over for everyone.

In this new reality, Wonder Woman trains with Ares, God of War.

The new version of Cassie joins the Teen Titans.

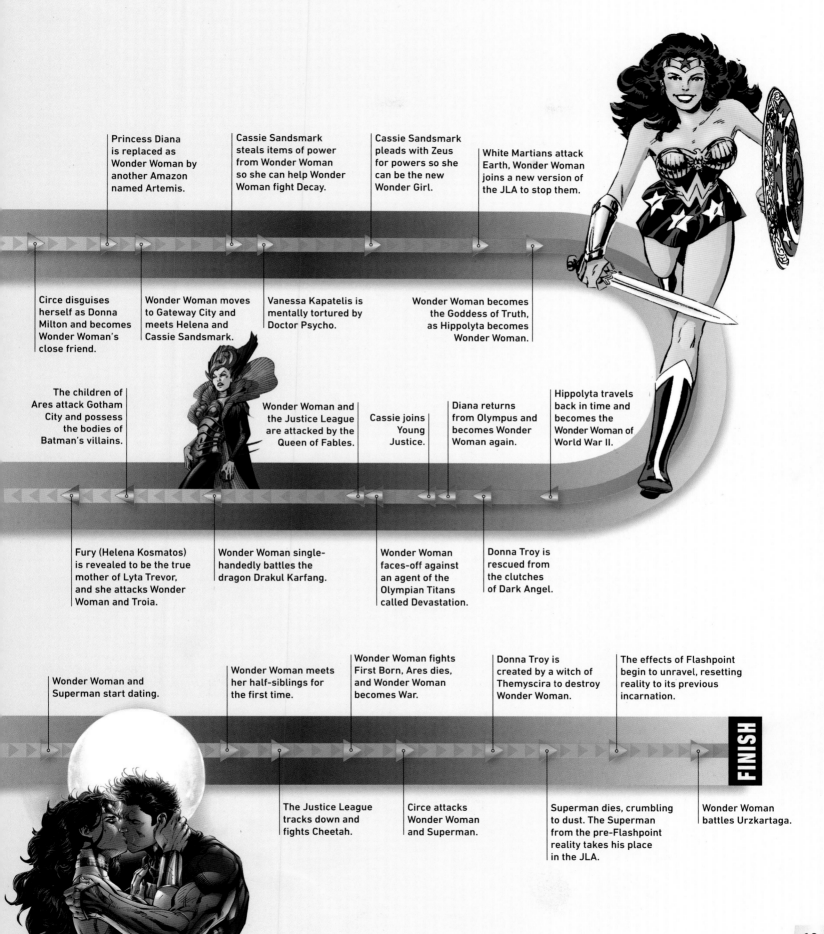

Princess Diana is replaced as Wonder Woman by another Amazon named Artemis.

Cassie Sandsmark steals items of power from Wonder Woman so she can help Wonder Woman fight Decay.

Cassie Sandsmark pleads with Zeus for powers so she can be the new Wonder Girl.

White Martians attack Earth, Wonder Woman joins a new version of the JLA to stop them.

Circe disguises herself as Donna Milton and becomes Wonder Woman's close friend.

Wonder Woman moves to Gateway City and meets Helena and Cassie Sandsmark.

Vanessa Kapatelis is mentally tortured by Doctor Psycho.

Wonder Woman becomes the Goddess of Truth, as Hippolyta becomes Wonder Woman.

The children of Ares attack Gotham City and possess the bodies of Batman's villains.

Wonder Woman and the Justice League are attacked by the Queen of Fables.

Cassie joins Young Justice.

Diana returns from Olympus and becomes Wonder Woman again.

Hippolyta travels back in time and becomes the Wonder Woman of World War II.

Fury (Helena Kosmatos) is revealed to be the true mother of Lyta Trevor, and she attacks Wonder Woman and Troia.

Wonder Woman single-handedly battles the dragon Drakul Karfang.

Wonder Woman faces-off against an agent of the Olympian Titans called Devastation.

Donna Troy is rescued from the clutches of Dark Angel.

Wonder Woman and Superman start dating.

Wonder Woman meets her half-siblings for the first time.

Wonder Woman fights First Born, Ares dies, and Wonder Woman becomes War.

Donna Troy is created by a witch of Themyscira to destroy Wonder Woman.

The effects of Flashpoint begin to unravel, resetting reality to its previous incarnation.

The Justice League tracks down and fights Cheetah.

Circe attacks Wonder Woman and Superman.

Superman dies, crumbling to dust. The Superman from the pre-Flashpoint reality takes his place in the JLA.

Wonder Woman battles Urzkartaga.

FINISH

THE CREATION OF A LEGEND

"As lovely as Aphrodite, as wise as Athena, with the speed of Mercury..."

At a time when muscled male Super Heroes battled through the underworld for the damsel in distress, concerns over effects of childhood exposure to this brand of brutality were emerging. Comic books were filled with male protagonists solving problems in a traditionally male manner. It was in this atmosphere that comics publisher Maxwell Charles Gaines grew concerned. Turning to noted psychologist Dr. William Moulton Marston—a believer in the "great educational potential" of comic books—for help, he sought to bring to life a Super Hero that would rely on compassion over violence. It was Marston's wife Elizabeth who pointedly declared that the character must also be a woman.

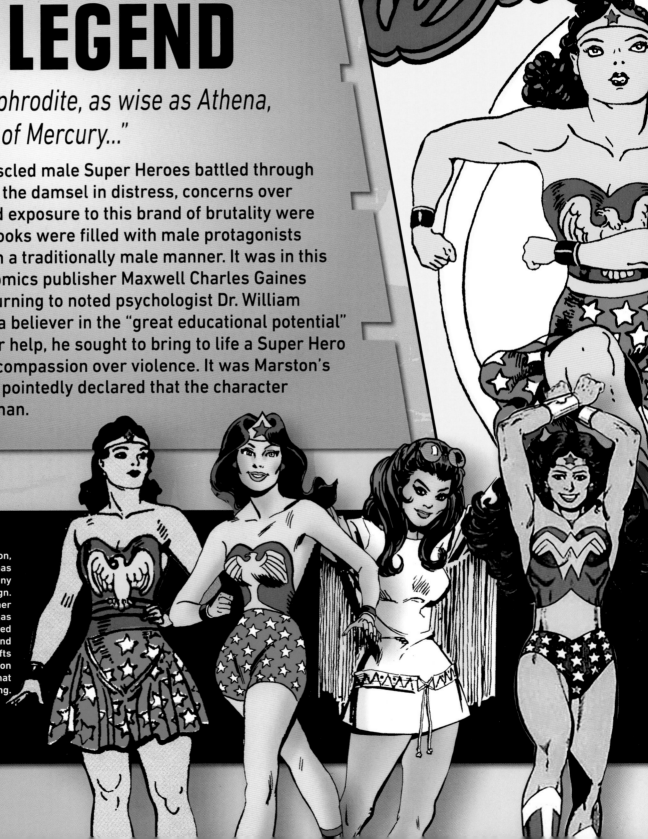

Since her creation, Wonder Woman has undergone many alterations in design. With each one, her visual style has adapted to the related era of publishing and the consequent shifts in public perception and fashion that changing times bring.

AT LAST, IN A WORLD TORN BY THE HATR[ED]... WARS OF MEN, APPEARS A <u>WOMAN</u> TO WHOM T[HE]... LEMS AND FEATS OF MEN ARE MERE CHILD['S]... A WOMAN WHOSE IDENTITY IS KNOWN TO N[O]... WHOSE SENSATIONAL FEATS ARE OUTSTAND[ING]... FAST-MOVING WORLD! WITH A HUNDRED T[IMES THE]... AGILITY AND STRENGTH OF OUR BEST MALE... AND STRONGEST WRESTLERS, SHE APPEARS... THOUGH FROM NOWHERE TO AVENGE AN... OR RIGHT A WRONG! AS LOVELY AS A[PHRODITE]... AS WISE AS ATHENA — WITH THE SPEED... [MER]CURY AND THE STRENGTH OF HERCULES... IS KNOWN ONLY AS **WONDER WOMAN**... SHE IS, OR WHENCE SHE CAME, NOBO[DY]...

TO BEGIN THE STRANGE HISTORY OF "WONDE[R]... US GO OUT OVER THE SEA AND FOLLOW I[N]... A PLANE, ENTIRELY OUT OF GASOLINE! AS... FLOUNDERS HELPLESSLY IN THE SKY, AND [THEN]... ON THE SHORES OF AN UNCHARTED ISLE... MIDST OF A VAST EXPANSE OF OCEAN...

TRADE MARK APPLICATION PENDIN[G]

DEBUT

Wonder Woman made her debut in the pages of *All-Star Comics* #8, published in 1941. An instant success, Wonder Woman served exactly the purpose Marston intended, showing the world the face of a strong and independent female Super Hero—one whose journey could parallel and chronicle the real-world growth in the power of women. Seventy-five years and thousands of stories later, Wonder Woman is still going strong, still inspiring and educating women and men of all ages.

WILLIAM MOULTON MARSTON

William Moulton Marston, born in Massachusetts, USA, spent the early part of his career studying the connections between emotions and the effects they have on blood pressure—research that later contributed to the invention of the lie detector. He worked on Wonder Woman until his death in 1947, at the age of 53.

H.G. PETER

The original artist who brought Marston's vision to life was Harry George Peter, commonly known as H.G. Peter. Originally a newspaper illustrator, Peter moved from California to New York in 1907, transitioning to comics work shortly before the creation of Wonder Woman. Like Marston, he was a vocal advocate of 20th century feminism. He worked on Wonder Woman until his death in 1958, at the age of 77.

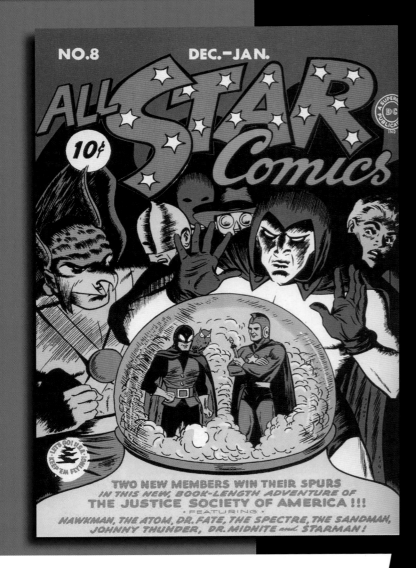

ALL-STAR COMICS
(VOLUME 1)
#8

THE STUNNING SECRET ORIGIN OF WONDER WOMAN IS REVEALED!

At the height of the Golden Age comes the demand for a new type of Super Hero, one that relies upon the powers of love and compassion over fists and fury. And so debuts Wonder Woman, proving that a woman can be just as heroic as any man!

DEC. 1941–JAN. 1942

MAIN CHARACTERS:
Wonder Woman • Hippolyta • Steve Trevor

SUPPORTING CHARACTERS:
Athena • Aphrodite • Mala • Von Storm • Fritz

MAIN LOCATION:
Paradise Island

1 Over a vast expanse of ocean, a small plane falls helplessly through the sky. Piloting the aircraft is Steve Trevor, captain in the US Army. Trevor has been in pursuit of an enemy spy bomber, but the long mission has left him out of fuel. His only hope is an uncharted isle below...

2 Trevor is gravely injured following a crash-landing. Luckily, two women—natives of the mysterious Paradise Island—discover him. One of them is the powerful Princess of the Amazons. Using her immense speed and strength, she rushes Trevor to the hospital of this advanced female society.

3 While contemplating the arrival of a man on Paradise Island, Queen Hippolyta is visited by the goddesses Athena and Aphrodite, who appear in a haze of mist. They command her to return Trevor to America, along with the strongest and wisest woman on Paradise Island—so helping the cause of justice and equality.

4 Hippolyta calls for a tournament to determine who will serve as the Amazon's emissary—but she forbids her daughter the Princess from entering. Soon it begins, and through each challenge, one woman stands well above the rest—a mysterious masked Amazon with black hair and a measure of speed and strength unmatched by all others.

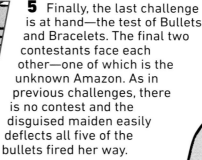

5 Finally, the last challenge is at hand—the test of Bullets and Bracelets. The final two contestants face each other—one of which is the unknown Amazon. As in previous challenges, there is no contest and the disguised maiden easily deflects all five of the bullets fired her way.

*"She shall go forth to fight for liberty and freedom of **all womankind!**"*

Hippolyta

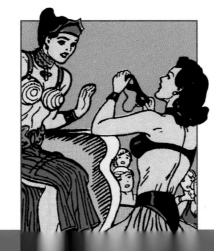

6 Hippolyta is shocked to discover that the victor is the Princess in disguise. Recognizing she has no choice, Queen Hippolyta grants her daughter a uniform for her mission. The Princess gives up her heritage and eternal life to become the champion of peace and love, known as Wonder Woman!

"We've seen what kind of **monsters** we create when **love** is denied."

Wonder Woman (Vol. 4) #35 (Nov. 2014)

"That's what **heroes** do—
they help those in need!"

Wonder Woman (Vol. 1) #184 (Oct. 1969)

"MAY THE GODS BE MERCIFUL TO ME!"

Wonder Woman (Vol. 1) #179 (Dec. 1968)

"YOU'LL FIND I CAN HOLD MY OWN."

Wonder Woman (Vol. 2) #208 (Nov. 2004)

"I'LL HIDE IN THIS PRETZEL!"

Wonder Woman (Vol. 1) #143 (Jan. 1964)

"You should know better than to stand in a lady's way!"

Sensation Comics (Vol. 1) #7 (Jul. 1942)

"Women and their children must no longer fear abuse, anywhere in this world."

Wonder Woman (Vol. 2) #170 (Jul. 2001)

"Aphrodite forbids us Amazons to let any man dominate us. *We are our own masters*."

Comic Cavalcade (Vol. 1) #8 (Sep. 1944)

"IT'S ABOUT TIME MEN LEARNED HOW CAPABLE WOMEN ARE."

Wonder Woman (Vol. 1) #30 (Jul. 1948)

"If it means interfering in an ensconced, outdated system, to **help** just one **woman**, **man,** or **child**... I'm willing to accept the consequences."

Wonder Woman (Vol. 2) #170 (Jul. 2001)

"THERE'S NOTHING IN THE WORLD SO DEAR AS CHILDREN."

Sensation Comics (Vol. 1) #7 (Jul. 1942)

"You are bound with the magic lasso —you must obey me!"

Sensation Comics (Vol. 1) #8 (Aug. 1942)

"WHY DID THEY BIND ME WITH SUCH SMALL CHAINS? IT'S AN INSULT!"

Sensation Comics (Vol. 1) #21 (Sep. 1943)

"Sorry Batman, but I'm not made of stone!"

Wonder Woman (Vol. 1) #212 (Jul. 1974)

"I'VE NEVER DISGUISED MYSELF AS AN ELEPHANT BEFORE..."

Wonder Woman (Vol. 1) #1 (Jun. 1942)

BATTLE ARMOR

At times of great need, Wonder Woman will forego her traditional Amazonian uniform, and instead wear the full armor of her people. Forged by the Amazon blacksmiths, this golden armor will turn any mortal blade.

EMBLEM

Reflecting the Aetos Dios—a giant golden eagle said to have served as a companion to the God Zeus—Wonder Woman wears this standard in respect of the Greek Gods that serve as patrons of her people. Designed with special care, the eagle on Princess Diana's uniform rests with its head bowed—representing one who will meet battle, but does not seek it.

STRAP

An occasional addition to the Amazon's outfit, the strap is useful for carrying the lasso or other weapons. With this simple but effective design, Wonder Woman can reach whatever she needs without distraction—essential in the heat of battle.

BELT

The decorative "W" shape of the belt buckle is a coincidence, as native Amazons neither speak nor write English. Their language is an infusion of ancient Greek with Afro-Asiatic influences and Indo-European roots. Regardless, with Wonder Woman's arrival in an English-speaking culture, it did not take long for the design to be associated with her initials.

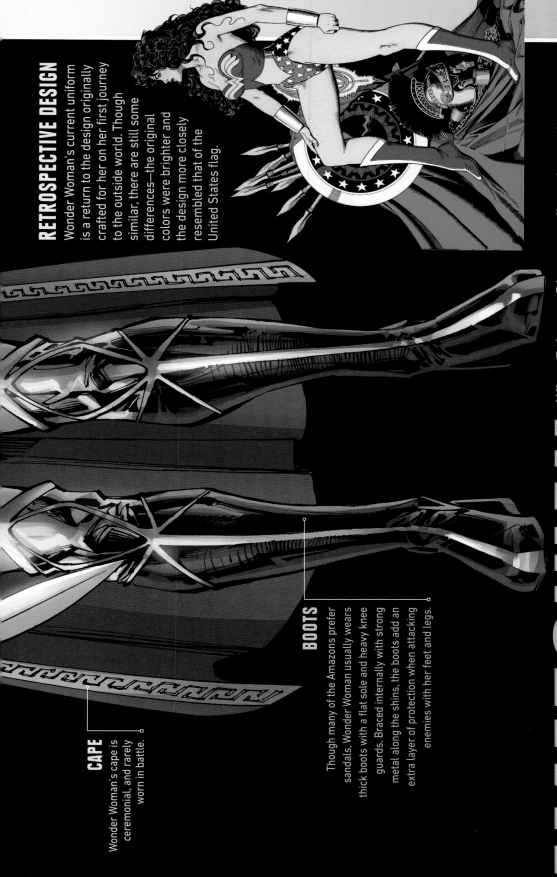

RETROSPECTIVE DESIGN

Wonder Woman's current uniform is a return to the design originally crafted for her on her first journey to the outside world. Though similar, there are still some differences—the original colors were brighter and the design more closely resembled that of the United States flag.

CAPE

Wonder Woman's cape is ceremonial, and rarely worn in battle.

BOOTS

Though many of the Amazons prefer sandals, Wonder Woman usually wears thick boots with a flat sole and heavy knee guards. Braced internally with strong metal along the shins, the boots add an extra layer of protection when attacking enemies with her feet and legs.

AMAZONIAN APPAREL

When Princess Diana was first chosen by the Olympian Gods to leave Themyscira as Wonder Woman, the Amazons created an outfit for her. It represented their culture and reflected the flag of the American soldiers whose plane had crashed upon their shores. Made of fabrics and metals more finely crafted than anything mortal hands could ever make, the Amazon Princess is well protected, yet mobile in battle.

PEACE THROUGH STRENGTH

Although her mission is one of peace, Wonder Woman's role as a champion of hope and liberator of the oppressed frequently brings her into conflict with the forces of evil. Luckily, the Gods have given the daughter of Themyscira the tools she needs to defend both herself and the world.

GOLDEN LASSO OF TRUTH

This was woven from the girdle belonging to the Earth Goddess, Gaea, and empowered by the fires of the Goddess Hestia. All beings bound by this unbreakable magical rope are compelled to speak only truths and obey commands.

Over the years, Wonder Woman has grown increasingly adept at wielding the Golden Lasso of Truth, and can deploy it like a whip, striking her targets with pinpoint accuracy. Due to the lasso's magical properties, it can extend to whatever lengths are required.

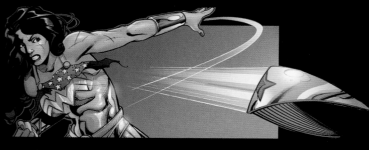

ROYAL TIARA

While many Amazons wear similar adornments, Princess Diana's tiara serves as both a badge of her royal station and an emblem of her role as Wonder Woman. It is forged of the same metals used in her uniform, and is virtually indestructible. Razor-sharp and magically enchanted, it can even cut through solid steel when thrown by Wonder Woman's strong hand.

ARMOR, SHIELD, AX, AND SPEAR

Amazon-forged and far stronger than any steel found in the world of men, these weapons and armor are used by Wonder Woman both in formal ceremony and during her most dire battles.

SWORD OF HEPHAESTUS

Gifted by the God of Blacksmiths, Wonder Woman carries her sword into battle only when the need is greatest. The blade is imbued with magic, and carries an edge so sharp that it can cut through any metal crafted by the hands of mankind, no matter how thick or strong it may be.

BULLETPROOF BRACELETS

These forearm guards are forged of an indestructible metal taken from the Aegis shield of Zeus. With these vambraces, Wonder Woman can block bullets, swords, and even energy attacks. All Amazons wear some form of bracelet of their own design—a decree by the Gods to never allow others to enslave them. This promise to the Gods is not made lightly, as without them, an Amazon will slip into a berserker rage.

Wonder Woman can slam her bracelets together, creating either an intense magical lightning strike or a powerful wave of concussive force. More recently, the Amazon warrior has been able to project swords of an unknown energy source from her gauntlets.

THE POWERS OF OLYMPUS

When Princess Diana was chosen to become the Amazons' emissary to the outside world, the Olympian Gods saw to it that their champion was granted the strength of body, mind, and spirit needed to achieve her mission.

SPEED OF LIGHTNING

Granted to Diana from the fastest god, Hermes, Wonder Woman can think faster, react quicker, and move with more speed than any normal mortal being. The powers of Hermes even give Wonder Woman the ability to fly, should the situation call for it.

STRENGTH OF THE WORLD

Wonder Woman's great strength was bestowed by Demeter, Goddess of the Land and the Harvest. Thanks to this divine gift, the Amazon's power is unmatched by any other native of the mortal world—and even rivals that of some of the Olympian Gods.

HUNTER'S INSTINCT

Through Artemis, Wonder Woman can hear a whisper miles away, and see across a city. Her sense of taste is so refined that she can detect every ingredient in a meal, and her sense of touch so nuanced she can trace an enemy's distant footsteps through the vibrations in the ground.

WISDOM OF THE ANCIENTS

The wisdom of Athena is Wonder Woman's to call upon. This gives the Amazon the deep insight she needs to make snap judgments even during the most dangerous predicament.

SISTERHOOD OF FIRE

The hearth fires of the Goddess Hestia give the Amazon Princess the ability to divine the truth in the hearts of those she encounters. Wonder Woman channels this skill through her unbreakable Golden Lasso of Truth, woven from the Golden Girdle of Gaea.

INNER BEAUTY

Through Aphrodite, Wonder Woman was given a boundless love and compassion for all life. This seemingly simple enhancement is what drives Wonder Woman's courage and selflessness. It pushes her heroism to its limits and gives her the emotional strength to risk her own life in service of others.

INVISIBLE JET

Wonder Woman's Invisible Jet has taken many forms over the course of the Amazon's crime-fighting career, but always serves the same purpose—allowing Wonder Woman to move undetected, quickly, and quietly. In this way it is possible for the Super Hero to arrive at the heart of a struggle, while avoiding any unnecessary conflict in the process.

Wonder Woman could control her plane telepathically in its earliest incarnations.

An invisible rope ladder extends from the hatch of the plane when opened.

Anything inside the plane is rendered invisible as well.

ORIGINAL

Built by the Amazons, the Invisible Plane responded to Wonder Woman's mental commands broadcast through her tiara. With a top speed of 2,000 miles per hour, the original Invisible Plane operated using a propeller and had room for extra passengers.

"Out of the blue hurtles a silent, transparent plane…"

Sensation Comics #1

ALIEN

Later on, Wonder Woman gained a new Invisible Jet. It was actually a shape-shifting, living, crystalline entity that had been altered by a subterranean culture called the Lansinarians. After discovering the plane was a living entity, Wonder Woman befriended it, and it transformed into a massive invisible floating sanctuary, called the Wonderdome.

STEALTH JET

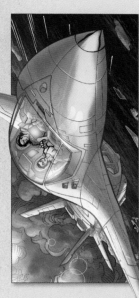

After the Wonderdome sacrificed itself to shield the East Coast of the United States from a massive tidal wave, Wonder Woman was gifted a state-of-the-art stealth jet from Batman. It was not truly invisible, but was able to avoid being detected in most circumstances.

UPGRADE

A second version of this aircraft soon appeared with a jet engine in place of the propeller. The Invisible Jet went through several upgrades while Wonder Woman used it, and was even capable of space flight when necessary. After being tinkered with by gremlins, a friendly AI was installed that became an ally to Wonder Woman.

INCARCERATION

After a long battle with the Superman clone known as Bizarro, Wonder Woman is chained. Critically injured, the Amazon warrior is still able to muster the strength to block incoming bullets, but requires the aid of a comrade to free her before she can continue her fight.

*"**Bound.** The **cruelest fate** to which an Amazon can be subjected."*

WONDER WOMAN

CHAINS OF THE MIND

Wonder Woman is captured by the Duke of Deception and believes herself to be chained. In fact, she is bound by her own unbreakable Golden Lasso of Truth and soon realizes she can access her powers even if she cannot free herself.

THE CHAINS OF OPPRESSION

Wonder Woman uses her powers to fight for justice and freedom, but there is one weakness that can limit her ability to do this, which is often referred to as "Aphrodite's Law." After the Amazons were enslaved by Hercules and chained by the wrists in heavy iron bracelets, Aphrodite decreed that any Amazon who allows themself to be similarly bound by men would temporarily lose the natural strengths innate in all women of Themyscira. For Wonder Woman, this is especially dangerous, as the Amazon loses not just her natural strength, but the great powers granted to her by the Olympian Gods.

AN UNSTOPPABLE MIGHT

At some point, Aphrodite's Law was overturned. Now Wonder Woman can break free of any mortal chain or shackle, regardless of the gender of the person who binds her. Still, the myth of the Amazon's secret weakness persists, leading male criminals to constantly underestimate her power.

CHAIN REACTION

Captured by Ares' henchman, Lord Conquest, Wonder Woman and Steve Trevor are chained. It is not the strength of the chains that makes her weep, but the fact that men have welded links to her Amazon bracelets—rendering her powerless.

THEMYSCIRA

The secret island of Themyscira is an ancient sanctuary for the Amazon race of female warriors, created for them by the Olympian Gods. The remote and mysterious island became the Amazons' home after they were enslaved by Hercules and his army. Led by Queen Hippolyta, the women freed themselves, turning on their attackers and vowing never again to live under man's oppressive rule. They abandoned their homes and journeyed to the island, where they continue to uphold the ideals of democracy, peace, and liberty.

The Themyscirans are a technologically advanced people who believe in and worship the ancient Greek gods. Many of them are trained as warriors, while others serve as scholars, architects, or healers. Themyscira was Wonder Woman's home, and when she left it to become its ambassador in the outside world, she cast off her immortality forever.

Enchanted Island
Known as "Paradise Island", Themyscira is rumored to be enchanted—if a man were to ever set foot upon its shores, the Amazons would lose their fabled immortality.

Socialism and Sisterhood

The Amazons have a dense population, numbering in the thousands. Despite this, the hidden island is abundant in both space and resources. Everyone has a role in this culture, and all are treated equally, with access to whatever they need.

Forever Vigilant

Though the island appears idyllic and peaceful, underneath the surface lies a rift to the realm of Hades, where untold horrors seek to spill out into the mortal realm. The Amazons monitor this gateway and use both magic and advanced technology to keep it sealed.

Art and Science

The sprawling city of the Amazons has been built and rebuilt over thousands of years. It contains a rich assortment of advanced cultural buildings, including a deep space observatory, an amphitheater, and multiple museums and libraries.

HIPPOLYTA

Queen of the Amazons and champion of liberty and equality, Hippolyta has ruled her people for thousands of years, often sacrificing her own happiness and desires for the greater good. It is a difficult balance for her to maintain, where each decision risks turning those she loves against her.

Motherhood

Her spirit craving the daughter that was never born, Hippolyta's wish is eventually fulfilled when she gives birth to Princess Diana, the future Wonder Woman. Accounts conflict on the true story of Hippolyta's pregnancy, with most of the Amazons (Wonder Woman included) believing that the Princess was sculpted from clay and granted life. In truth, Hippolyta was seduced by the Lord of the Gods, Zeus. Hippolyta kept this fact secret to spare the Amazons the wrath of Zeus' wife, Hera.

ORIGIN

Hippolyta's soul once belonged to a mortal cavewoman born thousands of years before the creation of the Amazons. Murdered by a man while pregnant, this unnamed woman's essence would become the template for Hippolyta's existence. Once she was granted a new life by the Olympian Gods, Hippolyta rose to the potential denied to her in her original incarnation, becoming the Queen of the Amazons, ruler of Themyscira. An immortal queen graced with wisdom, compassion, and absolute dedication for the Amazons, Hippolyta lacks only one thing in her life—the child she never had.

Liberation

Manipulated by Ares to attack the Amazons, Hercules and his army marched on the tribe. Unable to defeat them using their strength, Hercules turned to deception and drugging and enslaving the Amazon warriors. Hippolyta used her chains to break Hercules' neck and the women were freed through the grace of Athena. They found sanctuary on Themyscira.

"Cast off the yoke of man!"

HIPPOLYTA

NATURE AND NURTURE

Hippolyta may lack the god-granted superpowers that her daughter possesses, but the Queen is still one of the most formidable warriors of the island of Themyscira. Her speed and strength outweigh that of any mortal, and her great experience in battle makes her a tactician worthy of respect. In these ways, Hippolyta is a true leader and mother—not only to Wonder Woman, but to all Amazons.

DATA FILE

FIRST APPEARANCE: *All Star Comics* #8 (Dec. 1941–Jan. 1942)

OCCUPATION: Queen

AFFILIATIONS: Amazons, Justice Society of America, Justice League of America

POWERS/ABILITIES: Enhanced speed, strength, durability, immortality, exceptional fighter, tactician

ALTERNATES: In some parallel realities, Hippolyta is the daughter of Ares.

Hippolyta adopts a few tokens of her rank of queen—her tiara being one of them.

Though her hair is naturally black, Hippolyta has been known to change its color to blonde.

A skilled warrior and hunter, Hippolyta is proficient in the use of handheld weapons.

Leadership

Over the centuries, Hippolyta has taken many forms and lived many lives. She has walked in the mortal world as another incarnation of Wonder Woman. She has died and been resurrected, and she was transformed into stone. Hippolyta has been a warrior, a diplomat, a hero, and even very occasionally, a villain. But no matter what path Hippolyta might walk, one consistent truth is her unwavering love for her daughter, and for her people, the Amazons. Time and time again, the brave and loyal Hippolyta has proven she will fight for her people and that she is worthy of the title of queen.

OLYMPIAN GODS

The Olympian Gods are thought to have been born from a cascade of mystical energy known as the Godwave. This energy was a product of the Source—a multiversal consciousness beyond comprehension. The immortal and seemingly all-powerful Olympians exist as conceptual beings, with their very nature dependent on worship and perception. The Olympians were given their shape and form by the ancient Greeks, and much of that design has remained for millennia.

Zeus
Zeus is the Lord of the Olympians, the God of Lightning, and a prime advocate of the Amazons. He is known to be manipulative, so few fully trust his word.

Hera
Hera was one of the first to support the creation of the Amazons. Yet the Goddess of Marriage can be jealous, and has punished the Amazons for Zeus' wandering eye.

Poseidon
This God of the Sea helped the Amazons find their island home. Poseidon's interest in the warrior women is dependent upon his mood, and the needs of his older brother, Zeus.

Apollo
The God of Light and Truth, Apollo is revered by the Amazons. But like most of the other Olympian Gods, he can be fickle and can turn on his worshippers quickly and dangerously.

Artemis
Known as Diana, Wonder Woman is named after this Goddess of the Hunt. Her position as supporter of the Amazons has been usurped by her sister, Athena.

Athena
A true ally to the Amazons and Wonder Woman, the Goddess of Wisdom and Warfare is always present in Wonder Woman's life, even if only invisibly.

Ares
The God of War and Strife has no interest in peace, and as such has long opposed Wonder Woman's mission.

*"Thou wouldst speak thus to the **King of the Gods?**"*
ZEUS

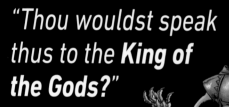

Demeter

One of the Goddesses to aid in the creation of the Amazons, the Goddess of the Earth and Harvest gifted the Amazons with fertile lands for agriculture.

Hephaestus

Mostly indifferent to the struggles of mortals or the squabbles of his siblings, Hephaestus nonetheless agreed to forge many of the armaments of Wonder Woman.

Hestia

Hestia is one of Diana's primary advocates. The Goddess of the Hearth and Home, it is Hestia's fires that empower the Golden Lasso of Truth that Wonder Woman has carried for so long.

Hermes

The messenger of the Gods, Hermes is a patron of the Amazons, but his support was temporarily lost after his body was destroyed in a war between the Olympian and Roman Gods.

Aphrodite

Although several Gods created the Amazons, it is often Aphrodite who receives the credit. She demanded that they wear the Bracelets of Submission to remind them against yielding to men.

Despite their great power, the immortal Olympians are flawed with an encapsulation of human emotion and expression. Consequently, they bicker, lie, cheat, and steal. They love, wage war, and feel fear. During one conflict, several Gods decided to create a race of humanity that would represent the best virtues of mortal life: the Amazons. This decision was not made unanimously, and so the Amazons have remained a point of manipulation and contention between warring factions of the Gods.

Spirit of Destruction

Seeking to entertain himself with smaller conflicts, the spirit of Ares once possessed the body of a petty criminal named Ari Buchanan. He used this identity to distribute dangerous, technologically advanced weaponry across a city, warring with Wonder Woman along the way.

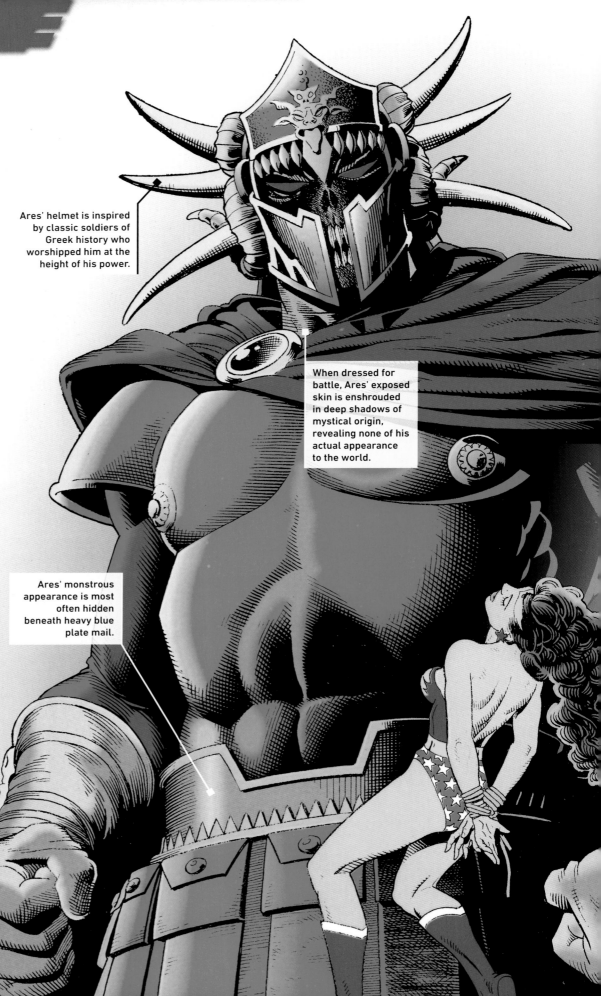

Ares' helmet is inspired by classic soldiers of Greek history who worshipped him at the height of his power.

When dressed for battle, Ares' exposed skin is enshrouded in deep shadows of mystical origin, revealing none of his actual appearance to the world.

Ares' monstrous appearance is most often hidden beneath heavy blue plate mail.

Wounds of War

While there are few beings as powerful as Ares, the War God is vulnerable to magical weapons. Even then, though, death is only temporary for Ares—a fact proven when Wonder Woman slayed the God with her battle-ax, and he returned from the dead shortly after.

DATA FILE

FIRST APPEARANCE: *Wonder Woman* (Vol. 1) #1 (Summer 1942) (as Mars)

OCCUPATION: God of War

AFFILIATIONS: Olympian Gods

POWERS/ABILITIES: Immortality, speed, strength, agility, control of the dead, telekinetic power of weapons, immunity to non-magical weapons, shapeshifting, teleportation

ALTERNATES: In an alternate reality, Ares is Wonder Woman's grandfather. Also uses aliases Mars, Ari Buchanan, and Tom Sera.

FACELESS FOES

Ares' form has evolved over the centuries to reflect the nature of war. Where once mortal beings battled each other face-to-face, now modern technology allows for wars to be fought remotely—with those locked in combat never seeing their enemy.

ORIGIN

The son of Zeus and Hera, Ares is a complex god, one who feeds off war, while at the same time requiring worshippers to survive the battlefield to build his shrines and temples. This conflict of interest might seem out of character for an iconic god, yet it is fitting that the God of War would not even find peace within his own nature.

Ares' appetite for destruction and chaos has led even his own parents to revile him. Not that Ares cares what the gods think of him. Instead, his interests lie with the manipulation of mortals; acts that have often brought the God of War into conflict with Wonder Woman.

*"Force is all men understand! Force is all they worship! And **I am force incarnate!**"*

ARES

Self-preservation

While Ares hungers for war and destruction, over the years he has learned that total annihilation of humanity would lead to his own ending. He has, therefore, challenged Wonder Woman and her allies to protect mankind from all threats—even those he poses himself.

ARES GOD OF WAR

Ares is a force of aggression and discord. He feeds off the conflicts of the mortal realm like a parasite. As humanity develops new and more potent ways to destroy, so the strength of the War God increases until few hold the power to stem the tide of Ares' bloodshed.

Classic Criminals

Priscilla Rich
This self-obsessed debutante's jealousy over Wonder Woman drove her to insanity. This madness manifested itself as the first incarnation of the murderous villain Cheetah!

Debbi Domaine
After Priscilla Rich died, her niece was brainwashed by the villain known as Kobra into adopting the mantle of Cheetah.

ORIGIN

Acting the role of friend to Wonder Woman when the Amazon first arrived in the world of mankind, Barbara Ann Minerva was in reality an ambitious and extremely selfish criminal. Her passion for archaeology led her into contact with a ceremonial blade tainted with blood of the Cheetah goddess. Using the blade to transfer the power of the goddess to herself, Minerva's own corrupt persona overwhelmed the spirit of the Cheetah. It took years for Wonder Woman to accept that her friendship with Minerva had been a lie and realize that her deadly arch-enemy was evil to the core.

"Barbara Minerva is dead. **There is only the Cheetah."**

CHEETAH

CHEETAH

Powered by a dark combination of ritual blood magic and the most ancient of sorceries, Barbara Minerva sheds her humanity at will and transforms herself into the deadliest of unnatural predators—the sinister super-villain known to the world as... Cheetah!

HONESTLY EVIL
Barbara Ann Minerva holds no faith in humanity. She believes that people are simply sheep waiting for the slaughter, and that she—as Cheetah—is the natural hunter. The strength of her convictions has been shown through her brutal actions and her chilling honesty while under the influence of Wonder Woman's Golden Lasso of Truth.

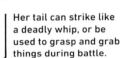

Her tail can strike like a deadly whip, or be used to grasp and grab things during battle.

Evil Upgrade
In the earliest days of Cheetah's criminal career, Minerva had to ingest a potion to trigger her transformation. After a visit from the sorceress Circe, Minerva's animal and human selves were permanently fused. As an added gift, Circe granted Minerva the ability to command the jungle cats from which she took her name.

Cheetah's senses are enhanced, meaning she can smell her prey from afar and track foes in absolute darkness.

DATA FILE

REAL NAME: Barbara Ann Minerva

FIRST APPEARANCE: *Wonder Woman* (Vol. 2) #7 (Aug.1987)

OCCUPATION: Archaeologist

AFFILIATIONS: Secret Society of Super-Villains

POWERS/ABILITIES: Cheetah's characteristics grant Minerva exceptional speed, agility, and enhanced senses. A brutal hand-to-hand combatant.

ALTERNATES: With each incarnation, Cheetah has become more savage and animalistic, even 'infecting' others with feline traits by biting them.

Her fangs are so sharp they can even pierce the durable flesh of a Super Hero.

Cheetah's claws are enchanted and can easily cut through layers of steel.

Sebastian Ballesteros

An agent of Circe, Ballesteros briefly stole the essence of Cheetah from Minerva, becoming the first male Cheetah in the process. During this time, Minerva found her access to her powers interrupted, and consequently battled and killed Ballesteros to reclaim the title of Cheetah.

Golden Age Gorilla

The original Giganta was a great ape that was hyper-evolved into a tall, red-haired woman. This newly created being sought to conquer and enslave humanity, starting with Wonder Woman and the scientist that transformed Giganta. She was ultimately defeated and sent to Paradise Island for reformation.

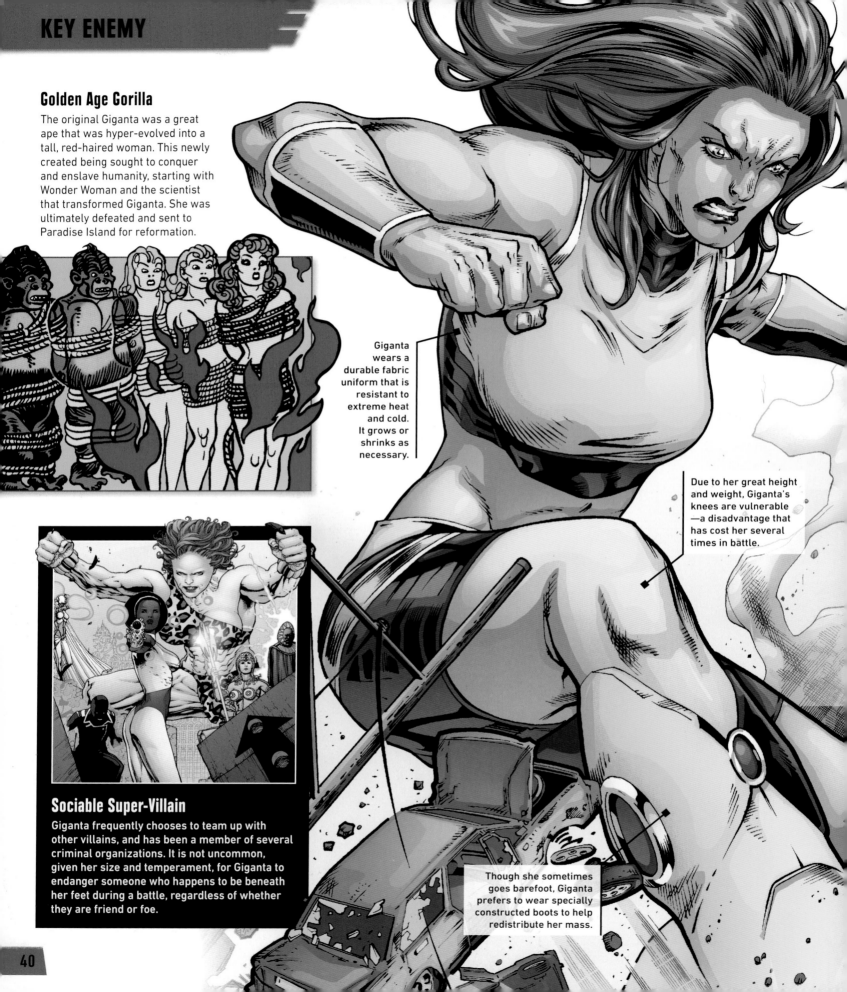

Giganta wears a durable fabric uniform that is resistant to extreme heat and cold. It grows or shrinks as necessary.

Due to her great height and weight, Giganta's knees are vulnerable —a disadvantage that has cost her several times in battle.

Sociable Super-Villain

Giganta frequently chooses to team up with other villains, and has been a member of several criminal organizations. It is not uncommon, given her size and temperament, for Giganta to endanger someone who happens to be beneath her feet during a battle, regardless of whether they are friend or foe.

Though she sometimes goes barefoot, Giganta prefers to wear specially constructed boots to help redistribute her mass.

MOSTLY EVIL

With no apparent limit to her size, Giganta is easily one of Wonder Woman's most formidable foes. Despite constant clashes with Super Heroes, however, Giganta is not particularly prone to violence for the sake of it. She is pragmatic and mercenary, primarily turning to criminal activities as a means to make money.

ORIGIN

A research scientist suffering from a fatal blood condition, Doctor Doris Zuel grew up teased and tormented by her peers. Despite her difficult childhood, Zuel hoped to help others like herself, and dedicated her brilliant mind to science. Over time, she developed a process that would save thousands of lives, but she was so desperate for a cure for her own condition that she tested her formula on herself before it was perfected. Zuel's body and mind were warped and her intellect was tragically decreased. She became Giganta, a villain driven by a rage that she cannot fully comprehend.

*"Don't take this the wrong way, but I **often** get the urge to **crush you in my grip**."*

GIGANTA

Big Romance

While teaching at Ivy University, Giganta began dating Ryan Choi, the fourth hero to be named the Atom. The relationship endured until Choi's death, after which Giganta sought revenge on his killer. Afterward, Giganta appeared to return to her criminal ways.

GIGANTA

One of Wonder Woman's earliest foes, Giganta is a scientific genius who can alter her powerful body to seemingly limitless heights. Add in her great strength and invulnerability, and it's no surprise that when Giganta appears on the scene, destruction quickly follows!

CIRCE

Circe has been sowing discord between women and men for millennia. Thwarted by Queen Hippolyta in her attempt to mutate Amazon boys into half-animal slaves called bestiamorphs, Circe saw Wonder Woman's arrival in the world of mankind as her best chance at revenge.

ORIGIN

Circe was the princess of the ancient kingdom of Colchis, but she was driven away after slaying her husband. The princess sought refuge on the island of Aeaea and prayed to the goddess Hecate for power. Hecate answered, and granted her own soul for Circe to use.

This power came with a prophecy: "Upon the death of witch and the birth of witch, Hecate, by name and choice, shall repossess her soul." Circe did not pay much attention to the prophecy and started a 3,000-year reign of terror—beginning with the total destruction of Colchis.

By the time Wonder Woman appeared, Circe had become a hermit, living on Aeaea with her bestiamorphs. She recalled the prophecy and realized that she might be the first witch named by Hecate long ago, and that Wonder Woman might be the second witch.

Best Frenemies

During a plan to defeat Wonder Woman, Circe transformed into a mortal—Donna Milton—and befriended her arch-nemesis. Circe's spell was so powerful that she forgot who she was and truly befriended her enemy—making Circe hate Wonder Woman more when she returned to her normal self.

Dear Daughter

While Circe was in her mortal form as Donna Milton, she became pregnant by Ares, God of War. Ares was not interested in fatherhood and tried to kill Donna. She survived and Wonder Woman helped deliver the baby. A grateful Circe named her Hippolyta, or "Lyta," after Wonder Woman's mother.

FIENDISH FLIRT

Despite her evil nature, Circe enjoys the more fun aspects of villainy, and often chooses to toy with her foes. Sometimes, the sorceress devises games and challenges for her enemies, just to see how they fair when pitted against her.

*"You are a god in **title only!**"*
CIRCE

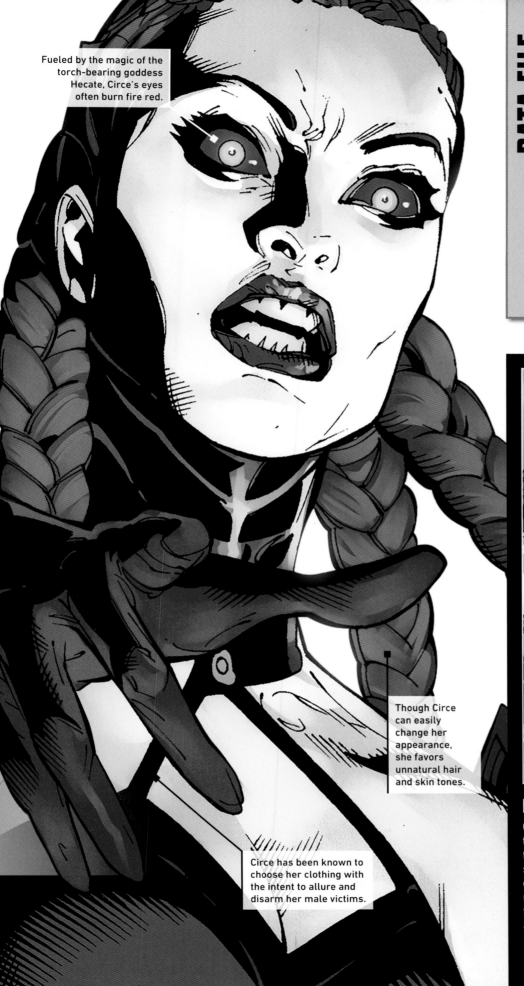

Fueled by the magic of the torch-bearing goddess Hecate, Circe's eyes often burn fire red.

Though Circe can easily change her appearance, she favors unnatural hair and skin tones.

Circe has been known to choose her clothing with the intent to allure and disarm her male victims.

DATA FILE

FIRST APPEARANCE: *Wonder Woman* (Vol. 1) #37 (Sep.–Oct. 1949)

OCCUPATION: Sorceress

AFFILIATIONS: Injustice Gang (formerly)

POWERS/ABILITIES: Seemingly immortal, Circe can manipulate reality through magic and transform mortals into bestiamorphs. She can alter minds, create illusions, and revive the dead.

ALTERNATES: Circe's expertise is the magic of transformation, and as such her appearance is often in flux. Her most significant trait is her hair color, which was purple pre-Flashpoint before changing to red.

Evil Transformations

Circe has taken great joy in using her powers of transformation to empower Wonder Woman's many foes. From enhancing the deadly Cheetah or the shape-shifter Everyman, Circe's handiwork is evident. No one is safe from the evil witch's masterful manipulations—and Wonder Woman finds herself haunted by Circe's cruel torment and torture of innocent beings.

Captain Wonder

Doctor Psycho once created a superpowered form for himself called Captain Wonder. The new super-villain was based on the fantasies of Wonder Woman's boyfriend, Steve Trevor. He was stronger, faster, and more powerful than Wonder Woman in every way.

ORIGIN

Edgar Cizko had endured a difficult childhood and had been the subject of severe bullying by his peers. After being admitted into high school at an unusually early age, Cizko found he had drawn the attention of the sinister organization, the Hierarchy of International Vengeance and Extermination—also known as H.I.V.E. Under the influence of the H.I.V.E. scientists, Edgar's enormous potential for power was unlocked, and the rage-filled young man became the super-villain called Doctor Psycho.

As Doctor Psycho, Cizko terrorized multiple lives, with a distinct preference for turning his twisted telepathic powers on women. It was inevitable that his cruel crimes would draw the attention of Wonder Woman.

> *"Killing's too good for a **woman!**"*
> DOCTOR PSYCHO

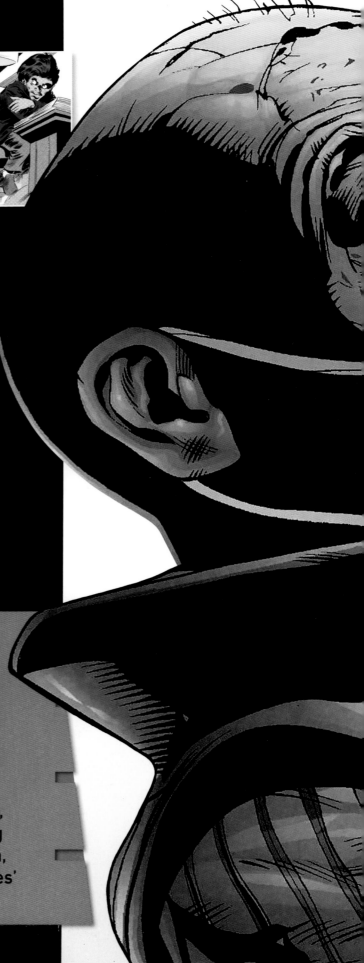

DOCTOR PSYCHO

A powerful telepath with a deep-seated hatred of women, Doctor Psycho is one of Wonder Woman's most disturbing and dangerous foes. He cares little about crime or wealth, instead using his vast mental abilities to enter his enemies' minds and torture them psychically for his own pleasure.

Doctor Psycho's forehead is covered with scars, a result of the H.I.V.E.'s experiments.

DATA FILE

REAL NAME: Edgar Cizko

FIRST APPEARANCE: *Wonder Woman* (Vol. 1) #5 (Jun.–Jul. 1943)

OCCUPATION: None

AFFILIATIONS: Secret Society of Super-Villains

POWERS/ABILITIES: One of the strongest telepaths on the planet, Doctor Psycho is capable of creating illusions so real they can kill.

ALTERNATES: Early appearances show Cizko to be dark-haired and diminutive. Post-Flashpoint, he is bald and uses bandages to cover his facial scars.

PSYCHIC ESTEEM

Doctor Psycho is incredibly self-conscious about both his height and his facial features. Consequently, he enjoys utilizing a variety of telepathic techniques to empower himself physically— often going so far as to borrow ideals of physical perfection from the minds of the women he has chosen to terrorize.

Doctor Psycho has taken to wearing a surgical mask.

Super Secret

During a battle with the Justice League, Doctor Psycho once came close to discovering Superman's secret identity. Luckily, the Martian Manhunter was able to use his own telepathic powers to erase the knowledge of Clark Kent from Doctor Psycho's mind.

Form of Fear

Early in his career, Doctor Psycho learned to use his mental powers to manipulate psychic energy and construct new forms of pure ectoplasm that could interact with the world on a physical level. Luckily, Psycho's ability to tap into this power was limited.

TRINITY

From the moment she steps off the island of the Amazons, Princess Diana has a new purpose in life—a mission to help the helpless, and fight for justice. Indeed, before long, Wonder Woman finds true allies to aid her in that quest. Heroes, who—though their methods may differ—stand true as her equals. The three super-heroic champions lead the path for others, inspiring like-minded people gifted with the skill and powers to stand against the tyrannical forces that constantly threaten freedom. Together they form a trinity, a physical representation of an iconic ideal—the mind, body, and soul of justice.

Superman's costume is a Kryptonian design. It adds extra protection to his near-invulnerable form.

Batman wields his trademark Batarangs with deadly accuracy and to lethal effect.

*"Kal looks to the **future**, Batman looks to the **past**... and I reside in the **present**, securely bridging the two."*

WONDER WOMAN

SUPERMAN

Strength, speed, and endurance—these abilities render Superman and Wonder Woman as true equals. In a world where few can match the raw power that either Super Hero has to offer, this common ground unites the pair. And yet, though they herald from such disparate backgrounds, time has proven that they have much to learn from one another as well.

Unlike her allies, Wonder Woman sees little need for extra body protection or to hide her identity.

BATMAN

The ever-grim Dark Knight might seem an odd companion for one whose light shines as brightly as Wonder Woman's. However, Batman's heroic fortitude, and his absolute and unyielding dedication to his cause, have won him the respect and admiration of the Amazon Princess a thousand times over—despite their many differences.

Conflicts

The path to justice is not always clear, and the three Super Heroes do not always see eye-to-eye on the methods to achieve it. While Batman's approach sometimes seems cruel or barbaric from the viewpoint of the Amazon emissary of peace, the Dark Knight forever has issues with Wonder Woman's willingness to take the life of an enemy in battle.

THE MULTIVERSE

There are many versions of Earth, and there are many versions of Wonder Woman. The Multiverse is infinite, and within it all things imaginable are possible.

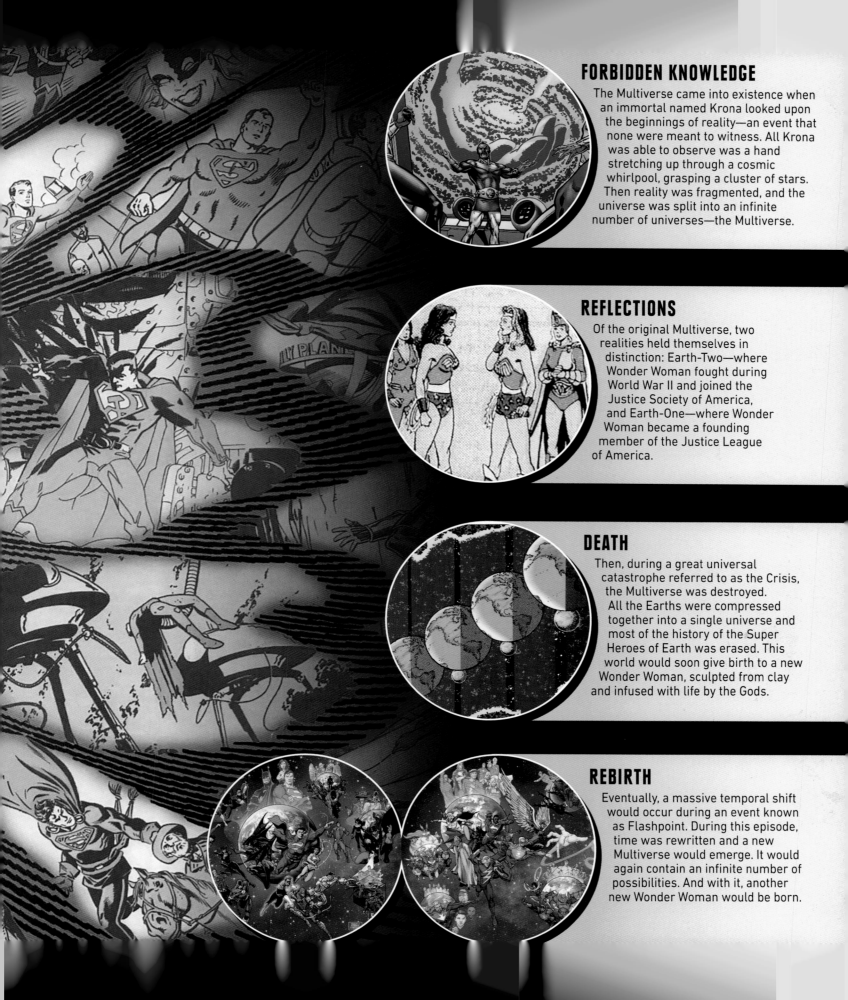

FORBIDDEN KNOWLEDGE

The Multiverse came into existence when an immortal named Krona looked upon the beginnings of reality—an event that none were meant to witness. All Krona was able to observe was a hand stretching up through a cosmic whirlpool, grasping a cluster of stars. Then reality was fragmented, and the universe was split into an infinite number of universes—the Multiverse.

REFLECTIONS

Of the original Multiverse, two realities held themselves in distinction: Earth-Two—where Wonder Woman fought during World War II and joined the Justice Society of America, and Earth-One—where Wonder Woman became a founding member of the Justice League of America.

DEATH

Then, during a great universal catastrophe referred to as the Crisis, the Multiverse was destroyed. All the Earths were compressed together into a single universe and most of the history of the Super Heroes of Earth was erased. This world would soon give birth to a new Wonder Woman, sculpted from clay and infused with life by the Gods.

REBIRTH

Eventually, a massive temporal shift would occur during an event known as Flashpoint. During this episode, time was rewritten and a new Multiverse would emerge. It would again contain an infinite number of possibilities. And with it, another new Wonder Woman would be born.

Shaped from clay and imbued with life from six Greek Gods, the original Wonder Woman stood as the pinnacle of female perfection. She represented an ideal for humanity to strive for, one whose original messages of social justice, equality, and peace still resonate today.

THE GOLDEN AGE

Wonder Woman (Vol. 1) #5 (Jun.–Jul.1943)
The sinister Doctor Psycho makes his
first appearance.

Wonder Woman (Vol. 1) #7 (Winter 1943)
A future is told where America has
a female president.

Sensation Comics (Vol. 1) #9
(Sep. 1942)
Wonder Woman meets the
real Diana Prince.

LIBERTY

Abandoning her royal heritage and her immortality, the Golden Age Wonder Woman stood as the emissary of the Amazon ideal—a symbol of liberty for women and men. Through her example, people who were suffering could find inspiration and hope for a future without fear and oppression.

EQUALITY

With her Golden Lasso of Truth, Wonder Woman is able to hypnotize millionaire department store owner Gloria Bullfinch into believing she is a poverty-stricken shop girl. By teaching Bullfinch a valuable lesson, Wonder Woman successfully fights for the dream of the liberated woman in the workplace, guaranteeing wage equality for the female employees.

Sensation Comics (Vol. 1) #8
(Aug. 1942)

JUSTICE

A former Holliday Girl, Lana Kuree, creates a formula designed to cure cancer. However, her fiancé—a killer and criminal—manipulates Kuree, making her believe that her medical experiments caused a man to die. Wonder Woman is able to liberate Dr. Kuree from this twisted romance, and reminds the young scientist not to let others try to control her.

Wonder Woman (Vol. 1) #17
(May–Jun. 1946)

DEMOCRACY

Using an Amazonian device known as the Magic Sphere, Wonder Woman looks one thousand years into the future. In this timeline, the United States of America exists as a near-utopian society where a woman will be elected president. Wonder Woman and her allies struggle against a treasonous uprising led by Senator Heeman of the Man's World Party—a group determined to oppress women.

Wonder Woman (Vol. 1)
#7 (Winter 1943)

FREEDOM

The fight for liberty takes many forms, but none so obvious as the desperate struggle taking place on the front lines of World War II. During this dark time, Wonder Woman embraces the role of an icon, abandoning her royal heritage and her immortality in the service of a cause she believes in. A true champion of liberty, Wonder Woman helps keep the shores of America safe from fascists, spies, and saboteurs by battling warmongering villains like Paula von Gunther and Doctor Poison.

Wonder Woman (Vol.1) #1 (Summer 1942)

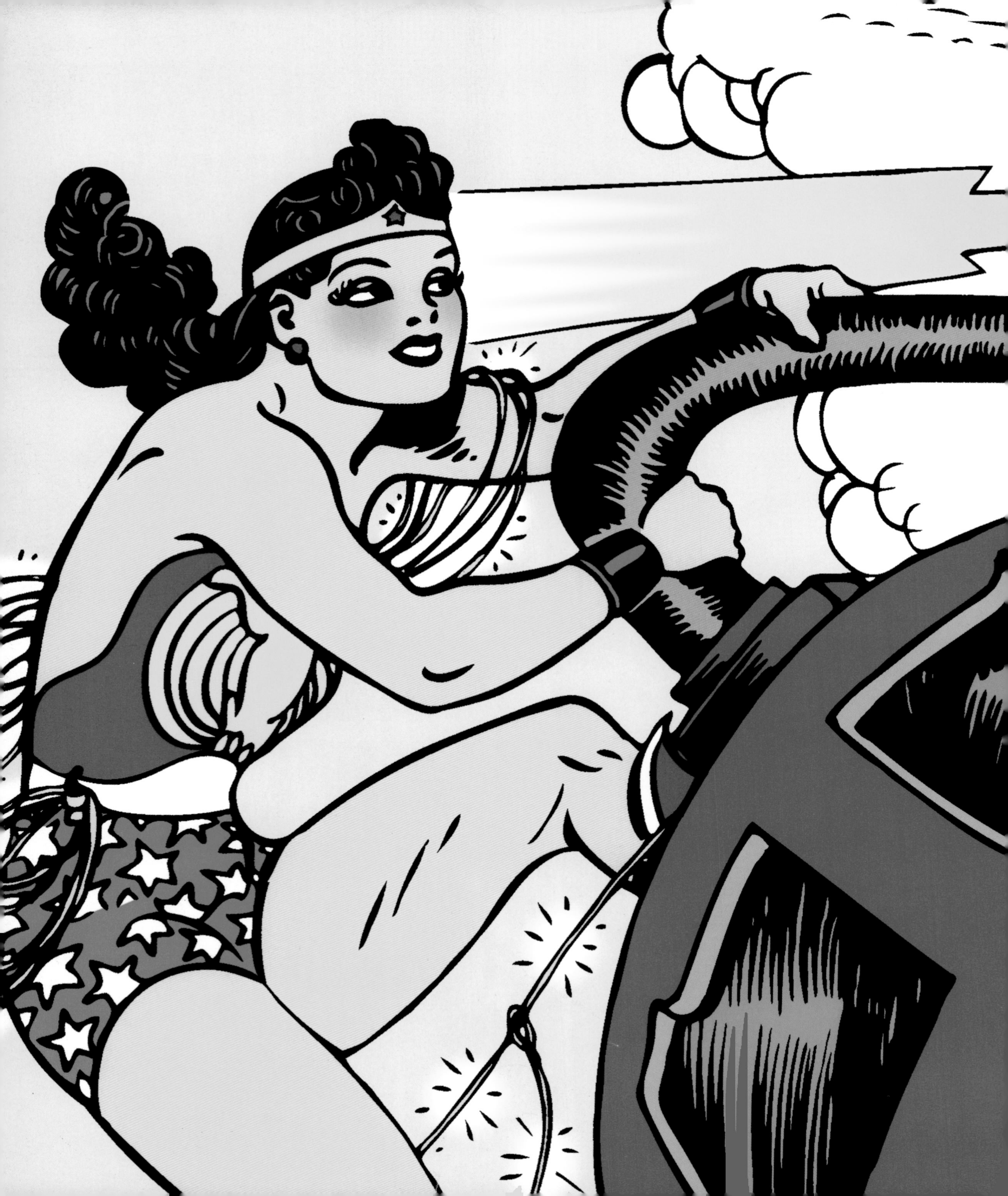

After lassoing the tail gun of an enemy bomber, Wonder Woman turns the tables on the sinister Hypnota and a Saturnian assassin, ending two terrible threats at once.

Wonder Woman (Vol. 1) #11 (Winter 1944)

A Hero in the Kitchen

Not only is Steve Trevor comfortable on the battlefield, he has a progressive attitude toward the dynamic of the household. When suddenly finding himself living in the golden age of humanity —a world where men share the chores of cooking and cleaning—he takes to this new role with a smile.

Steve's hair is naturally blond. It is a bit longer than standard regulations for his rank.

A true patriot, Steve often wears his military uniform, even when off-duty.

CREDIT WHERE CREDIT IS DUE

Confident in his role as Wonder Woman's friend and ally, the army captain never has a problem giving credit to the wonderful guardian angel for her heroics. Steve is always ready to ensure that the amazing Amazon— who has saved him and many others from peril countless times—is recognized for her heroism.

DATA FILE

FIRST APPEARANCE: *All Star Comics* (Vol. 1) #8 (Dec. 1941–Jan. 1942)

OCCUPATION: Military intelligence officer, Captain

AFFILIATIONS: US Army

POWERS/ABILITIES: Highly trained army officer, expert combatant

ALTERNATES: Steve Trevor has been killed and resurrected many times and has even taken a different name, Steve Howard.

The Power of Friendship

Though he is oblivious to Wonder Woman's true identity, and harbors no romantic interest in Diana Prince, Steve still considers his secretary to be a great friend. Despite underestimating Diana on more than one occasion, Steve is driven by genuine affection and compassion for his coworker.

Despite his frequent need to be rescued by Wonder Woman, Steve is quite capable in a fight.

STEVE TREVOR

The first man to ever find his way to Paradise Island would soon become Wonder Woman's true love. Steve Trevor is daring and bold, but not afraid to recognize the power of a strong woman. He is Wonder Woman's equal in spirit, and a supporter of her mission of peace and equality.

ORIGIN

A military intelligence officer in the United States Army Air Corp, Captain Steve Trevor's life took an exciting and strange turn when he was captured by enemy spies and locked within a remote-controlled plane. Managing to take control of the plane from within, Steve pursued the enemy, until eventually he found himself lost over the sea. He crash-landed the plane on Paradise Island—home of the mighty Amazons.

Weak and delirious from his injuries, Steve briefly woke during his flight back to the United States inside Wonder Woman's Invisible Jet. Spotting the Amazon in front of him, he thought he was seeing an angel. Then, overwhelmed and exhausted, Steve passed out. Wonder Woman decided to keep a close eye on the captain, posing first as his nurse, and later as his secretary, under the guise of Diana Prince.

"I really don't deserve this—all the credit belongs to Wonder Woman!"

STEVE TREVOR

No Time for Sexism

Even for someone as forward-thinking as Steve Trevor, some biases are deeply ingrained and take time to change. Luckily, Steve has the constant reminder of Wonder Woman around him to help pull him out of his few old prejudices.

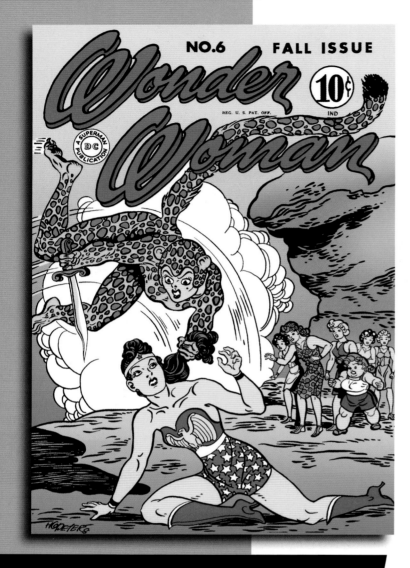

FALL 1943

MAIN CHARACTERS:
Wonder Woman • Priscilla Rich/Cheetah • Etta Candy • Steve Trevor

SUPPORTING CHARACTERS:
Courtley Darling • Detective Casey • Inspector Duncan

MAIN LOCATIONS:
The 400 Club • Capital Grain Co.

WONDER WOMAN
(VOLUME 1)
#6

INTRODUCING THE DEADLIEST PREDATOR THE WORLD HAS EVER KNOWN...

There is nothing so dangerous in the world as a villain driven by self-loathing and jealousy. One such character is Priscilla Rich, once a wealthy socialite, and now a psychotic criminal ruled by unrestrained rage and a split personality.

1 At a fund-raising performance, the theater audience is eager to see Wonder Woman demonstrate her powers. Hooded and bound by heavy chains, Wonder Woman is immersed in a water tank. Priscilla Rich, a jealous debutante, secretly binds Wonder Woman's wrists with her Golden Lasso of Truth. Luckily, the Amazon is able to reach the knotted lasso with her toes, and escapes just in time!

2 After Wonder Woman escapes this underhanded attempt at murder, Priscilla Rich is in a rage. At the height of her anger she looks into a nearby mirror, and within the reflective surface she sees a figure that is not quite her own, dressed in a costume of a cheetah.

*"**Death** is too good for her— I have a better plan!"*

PRISCILLA RICH, CHEETAH

3 Commanded by the reflection in the mirror, Priscilla Rich fashions herself a Cheetah costume. She then steals a hundred thousand dollars in charity earnings from the safe belonging to event organizer Courtley Darling. Cheetah tracks down Wonder Woman and, rather than kill her, plants the stolen money beneath her bed.

4 Cheetah's attempt to frame both Darling and Wonder Woman is only partially successful. Wonder Woman selflessly takes the blame for the crime, exonerating Darling in the process. Her rage unabated, Cheetah kidnaps Darling and arranges Wonder Woman's bail, knowing that the Amazon will trace her—and fall right into a death trap!

5 Buried in a vast bin of wheat grain, Wonder Woman uses all her strength to escape with the unconscious Darling. Meanwhile, Steve Trevor and Etta Candy, concerned for their friend, find the address Cheetah had used to arrange Wonder Woman's bail.

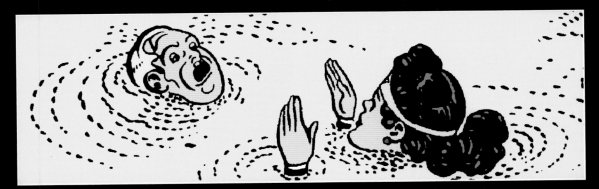

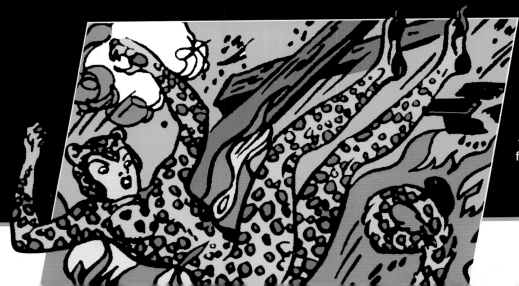

6 Attempting to destroy Wonder Woman and her friends, Cheetah sets fire to the warehouse. While the heroes manage to escape the burning building, Cheetah herself is caught within the perils of her own trap, apparently falling to her death within the flames she herself had created!

THE JUSTICE SOCIETY OF AMERICA

Shortly after arriving from Paradise Island, Wonder Woman joins the most powerful heroes of the 1940's as they gather together to defend innocents against the Axis forces. The team is named the Justice Society of America (JSA)—dedicated to fighting for the ideals of democracy.

CURE FOR THE WORLD

Earth-Two's Wonder Woman finds herself fighting against prejudice alongside Dr. Mid-Nite, Spectre, Hawkman, Starman, the Atom, and Johnny Thunder.

SPECTRE

Murdered while on a drive with his fiancée, Jim Corrigan's spirit found itself barred from the afterlife and returned to the mortal plane as an instrument of vengeance against criminals.

HOURMAN

Rex Tyler developed a special vitamin that gave the Super Hero enhanced strength and stamina for an hour at a time. With this, he became Hourman, a founding member of the JSA.

DOCTOR FATE

Kent Nelson caught the interest of the Lord of Order known as Nabu the Wise. The entity taught the mortal to fight supernatural evil as the golden-helmeted hero named Doctor Fate.

JOHNNY THUNDER

A comedic goofball, Johnny's claim to fame is his control over a mystical genie named Thunderbolt.

ALL-STAR SQUADRON

Under the guidance of President Franklin Roosevelt, members of the JSA joined with other heroic super-teams to form the All-Star Squadron—an official organization of Super Heroes charged with defending America during World War II.

SANDMAN

One of the earliest so-called "mystery men," Wesley Dodds is also known as the Sandman. He wears a World War I gas mask and wields a sleep-inducing gas gun as he cleans up crime and corruption.

THE FLASH

After toxic fumes gave Jay Garrick the power of super-speed, the teen college student became the first speedster to call himself the Flash—the hero of Keystone City.

WILDCAT

A highly skilled boxer who has literally been granted nine lives, Ted Grant took inspiration from Green Lantern and created a catsuit in which to fight crime.

HAWKMAN

A reincarnated Egyptian prince, Carter Hall created a set of gravity-defying wings for himself and his girlfriend. Together they became the crime-fighting duo of Hawkman and Hawkgirl.

DOCTOR MID-NITE

Blinded by a grenade, Charles McNider soon discovered that he could see perfectly well in absolute darkness. Using so-called "blackout bombs" and a special visor, he fights crime as Doctor Mid-Nite.

GREEN LANTERN

Alan Scott discovered a mystical green lantern when working as a construction engineer. Making himself a ring out of it, Scott began a long career as the energy-wielding Green Lantern.

THE ATOM

At only five feet one inch tall, Al Pratt decided the best defense was a good offense, and trained his body to the peak of physical fitness.

DIANA PRINCE—SECRET IDENTITY!

Seeking to keep close to Steve Trevor and the troubles that seem to surround him, Wonder Woman devises a means by which to keep her identity hidden in the world outside Paradise Island—a secret identity!

"What an amazing coincidence—I'm Diana too!"
THE ORIGINAL DIANA PRINCE

Sensation Comics (Vol. 1) #1 (Jan. 1942) *Wonder Woman earns a living on stage while finding her place in Man's World.*

SHOW BUSINESS

While Steve Trevor recovers from the injuries he incurred when his plane crashed on Paradise Island, Wonder Woman—newly arrived in the United States—takes a job on stage blocking bullets with her bracelets. Her fame spreads and she earns a lot of money. However, she abandons it all when Steve recovers.

Sensation Comics (Vol. 1) #3 (Mar. 1942) *On her first day on the job, Diana Prince makes a rival.*

PRINCESS MEETS PRINCE

Wondering how she can manage to stay near Steve without drawing too much attention to herself, Wonder Woman encounters a nurse named Diana Prince, who happens to be a doppelgänger of the Amazon Princess. When Wonder Woman learns that Diana needs a large sum of money to move away and marry her fiancé, she gives the nurse the cash. With permission, she then borrows Diana Prince's identity.

Sensation Comics (Vol. 1) #1 (Jan. 1942) *Wonder Woman encounters a broken-hearted woman in need.*

CAREER PATH

As Steve begins to recover, he no longer needs a nurse. Not wanting to let the soldier out of her sight, the new Diana Prince applies for a job as a secretary to Steve's boss, Colonel Darnell. Diana gets the job, but Steve's secretary, Lila Brown, does not take to her new coworker. Covering for her younger sister who is a Nazi spy, Lila frames Diana for treason. Wonder Woman exposes Lila's sister and the Amazon's secret identity remains safe.

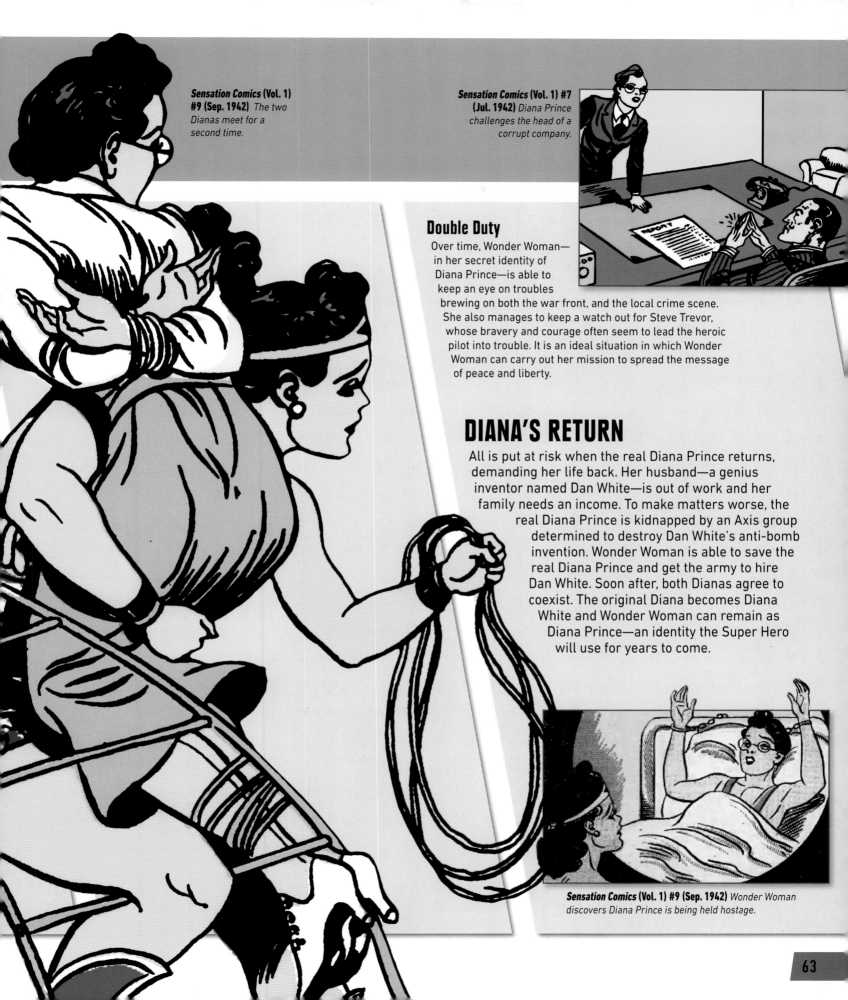

Sensation Comics (Vol. 1) #9 (Sep. 1942) *The two Dianas meet for a second time.*

Sensation Comics (Vol. 1) #7 (Jul. 1942) *Diana Prince challenges the head of a corrupt company.*

Double Duty

Over time, Wonder Woman— in her secret identity of Diana Prince—is able to keep an eye on troubles brewing on both the war front, and the local crime scene. She also manages to keep a watch out for Steve Trevor, whose bravery and courage often seem to lead the heroic pilot into trouble. It is an ideal situation in which Wonder Woman can carry out her mission to spread the message of peace and liberty.

DIANA'S RETURN

All is put at risk when the real Diana Prince returns, demanding her life back. Her husband—a genius inventor named Dan White—is out of work and her family needs an income. To make matters worse, the real Diana Prince is kidnapped by an Axis group determined to destroy Dan White's anti-bomb invention. Wonder Woman is able to save the real Diana Prince and get the army to hire Dan White. Soon after, both Dianas agree to coexist. The original Diana becomes Diana White and Wonder Woman can remain as Diana Prince—an identity the Super Hero will use for years to come.

Sensation Comics (Vol. 1) #9 (Sep. 1942) *Wonder Woman discovers Diana Prince is being held hostage.*

ETTA CANDY
& THE HOLLIDAY GIRLS

Wonder Woman's best friend throughout all her earliest adventures, Etta is a candy-eating, hard-punching, super-sassy sorority girl. She aids Wonder Woman in her many adventures and leads the girl brigade of Holliday College, known as the Holliday Girls.

> *"America's first women's expeditionary force!* **One hundred beautiful, athletic girls—like me!"**
>
> ETTA CANDY

Body Positive

Etta proves over and over again that she can keep up with her hero, never letting down Wonder Woman and never apologizing for being who she is.

Mental Communications

Etta Candy and the Holliday Girls are always ready for action! Whether fighting Nazis, traveling to alien worlds, or journeying through time, Etta and her sorority sisters are happy to help out. They answer Wonder Woman's call through the telepathic radio—a device capable of receiving the Amazon's own thoughts.

ORIGIN

Originally a sickly and malnourished young woman, Etta found her health bounce back after her appendix was removed and the girl gave in to her deep indulgences of candy. On a perpetual sugar rush, the supercharged Etta came to Wonder Woman's aid against the menace of Doctor Poison. She enlisted one hundred women to form an army ready to march against the guns of chemically brainwashed American soldiers. Distracting the men while Wonder Woman saved Steve Trevor and captured Doctor Poison, Etta Candy and her army jumped to the call and apprehended the mind-controlled male soldiers.

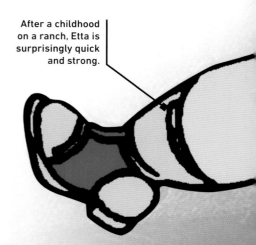

After a childhood on a ranch, Etta is surprisingly quick and strong.

Through Thick and Thin

There are a great number of loyal and dedicated Holliday Girls, including Virginia True, Glamora Treat, Faith Alden, Thelma Tall, Arda Prosperous, and Tina Toy. Unfortunately, some members let down the team: Wanta Wynn, whose competitive drive led to a form of temporary insanity, and Tress Akter, who, through jealousy, kidnapped a fellow actress. Regardless, Wonder Woman is always there for the team, through the good times and the bad times.

FAMILY MATTERS

A native Texan, Etta Candy was raised with her brother, Mint, on a ranch in Brazos County by her parents—Hard and Sugar Candy. Although the tough-as-nails, sassy sidekick has dated more than one man—even briefly becoming engaged— Etta is always very clear: She loves eating candy and being herself, more than she cares about someone loving her.

Etta often wears a variation of the Holliday College school uniform.

Etta's shorts are taken from the Holliday College marching band outfit.

DATA FILE

NAME: Etta Candy

FIRST APPEARANCE: *Sensation Comics* (Vol. 1) #2 (Feb. 1942)

OCCUPATION: College student

AFFILIATIONS: Beeta Lambda Sorority at Holliday College

POWERS/ABILITIES: Being awesome

ALTERNATES: In a later incarnation, Etta Candy is an African American working with the US military.

CRUEL VILLAINS

As a counter to the compassionate nature of the Golden Age Wonder Woman, many of the villains of this era have two notable traits in common: an unquenchable thirst for conquest, and a passion for immense cruelty.

BARONESS PAULA VON GUNTHER

Paula von Gunther was a Nazi spy and a talented inventor, who was known for enslaving and brainwashing people. Over the years, her criminal activities put her in conflict with Wonder Woman, until von Gunther was committed to the Amazons' Transformation Island. There, she renounced her evil ways and became an ally to the forces of good.

QUEEN CLEA

Queen Clea was the dictator of a submerged kingdom named Venturia. She coveted the neighboring undersea territory of Aurania—ruled by her rival, Queen Eeras. Wonder Woman intervened against the Queen's bid for power and saw to it that Clea was dethroned. In the absence of the dictator, a new ruler was elected— Octavia, daughter of Eeras. Clea would return many times to try to reclaim the throne, recruiting some of Wonder Woman's most dangerous foes on the way.

DOCTOR POISON

Doctor Poison was an Axis spy who disguised herself as a man. She was an expert in chemical research and used her talents to undermine the military efforts of the United States. As a preface to her attack on a military base, Doctor Poison kidnapped both Steve Trevor and Diana Prince, intending to interrogate the pair on the activities of the American forces. Once she was certain that her plan had not been compromised, Doctor Poison released a drug, named Reverso, into the water supply, creating chaos within the American camp. With the help of Etta Candy and the Holliday girls, Doctor Poison was defeated.

EVILESS

A ruthless slave driver from the planet Saturn, Eviless aided the Saturnian forces in their attempted conquest of Earth, capturing and torturing Steve Trevor in the process. The Saturnians were soon repelled. Eviless would return, beseeching Wonder Woman for sanctuary from the wrath of Duke Mephisto Saturno, who would not be pleased with the failure of his subjects. Eviless was given a chance to reform, but rejected it, escaping to plague Wonder Woman once more.

HYPNOTA

A villainess who posed as a male stage magician, Hypnota used a blue energy that emanated from her eyes to mesmerize any subject. She sought to provide the forces of Saturn with helpless, hypnotized slaves. When the war between Saturn and Earth ended, Hypnota tried to use her influence to reignite the conflict. Fortunately, Wonder Woman was able to thwart her efforts and she was sent to Transformation Island, where she remained unrepentant.

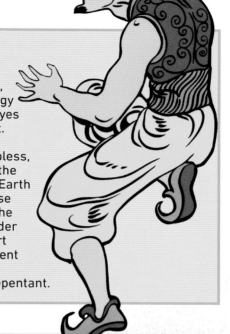

ZARA

The High Priestess of the Cult of the Crimson Flame, Zara used pyrotechnics combined with trickery and illusion to make her cult a worldwide phenomenon. This activity was aided by Zara's apparent ability to induce illness in any cult member who defied her. This power was eventually revealed to be psychosomatically induced by her illusions. Wonder Woman tried to reform Zara, but there was too much rage in the criminal for her to ever change her ways.

THE BLUE SNOWMAN

A school teacher named Byrna Brilyant used the likeness of a snowman and an invention by her late father to terrorize and blackmail her community. Byrna's father had created a "blue snow" that froze everything it touched. Brilyant's plan involved freezing the much-needed crops of Fair Weather Valley, and forcing the farmers to pay a fee for the antidote. Defeated in her mountain lair by Wonder Woman, the Blue Snowman was given a second chance at life on Transformation Island.

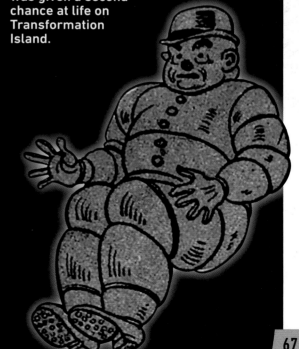

DUKE OF DECEPTION

A servant of Ares, the God of War, Deception was the very embodiment of evil and treachery. Wonder Woman faced the Duke on numerous occasions, and was frequently haunted by Deception's powers of illusion and mind control. The Duke took great delight in spreading falsehood and lies designed to ignite the conflicts of war. Little is known about the Duke's origins; it is generally assumed that he is a minor deity uplifted by the God of War to spread intolerance and confusion.

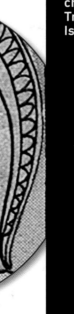

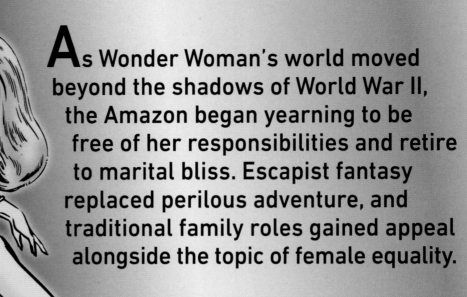

As Wonder Woman's world moved beyond the shadows of World War II, the Amazon began yearning to be free of her responsibilities and retire to marital bliss. Escapist fantasy replaced perilous adventure, and traditional family roles gained appeal alongside the topic of female equality.

THE SILVER AGE

Wonder Woman (Vol. 1) #107 (Jul.1959)
Wonder Girl faces three challenges
in order to claim her uniform.

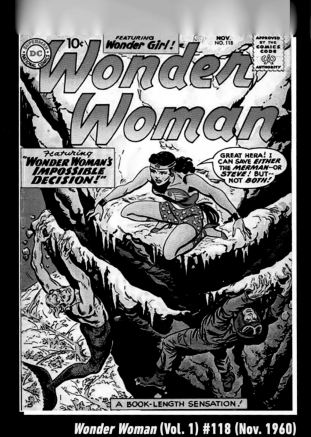

Wonder Woman (Vol. 1) #118 (Nov. 1960)
Which of the Amazon Princess'
loves will she rescue?

**Wonder Woman (Vol. 1) #136
(Feb. 1963)**
Wonder Woman is transformed
into a giant.

LOVE

World War II is over and the soldiers return home to their sweethearts. Love is in the air! In this Silver Age it is often implied that a woman—even a Wonder Woman—will never be complete without settling down to marry a strong man. Though Steve Trevor is Diana's true love, the Amazon is also wooed by other suitors.

BATTLE OF THE BOYFRIENDS

Eternally jealous, Steve Trevor demands that Wonder Woman fly him to Paradise Island so he can meet his rival—the aquatic half-fish being known as Mer-Man. The two men compete to prove which of them loves the Amazon more, while the Princess of Paradise Island is captured by a strange invader from another world.

Wonder Woman (Vol. 1) #125 (Oct. 1961)

HONEYMOON WORRIES

Having been knocked unconscious, a smitten Steve Trevor dreams of what life married to Wonder Woman might be like. Despite his desire to make the Amazon his bride, Steve's adoration turns to frustration when he imagines a honeymoon where his new bride has no time for him, and can't cook!

Wonder Woman (Vol. 1) #127 (Jan. 1962)

SUPER DATE

Wonder Woman, in her secret identity as Diana Prince, is fed-up with being passed over by an oblivious Steve Trevor for her heroic self. To get revenge on him for his desire for a platonic relationship, Wonder Woman stages a series of magical mirrors to transform her appearance, then goes on a date with Superman while disguised as Diana Prince.

Wonder Woman (Vol. 1) #130 (May 1962)

WINGS VERSUS FINS

On her way to the annual ceremony to retain the title of Wonder Woman, the Princess finds herself in a tug-of-war between two of her mythical male suitors: Mer-Man and Bird-Man. Each vies for the Amazon Princess' attention and distracts Wonder Woman from the threat of a living volcano that is attacking Paradise Island.

Wonder Woman (Vol. 1) #154 (May 1965)

PERSISTENT PROPOSALS

Will they or won't they? It is the question of the day as the most powerful woman on Earth battles to balance the dream of a happy home life with the responsibilities of a hero. And although she desperately loves Steve Trevor, the Princess of Paradise Island is all too aware that marrying a man would mean letting go of her role as champion and emissary of the Amazons for all time. Not that this stops Steve Trevor from his endless displays of affection. Steve's proposals are as bountiful as Wonder Woman's strength, and Diana loves him all the more for his persistence.

Sensation Comics (Vol. 1) #97 (Jun. 1950)

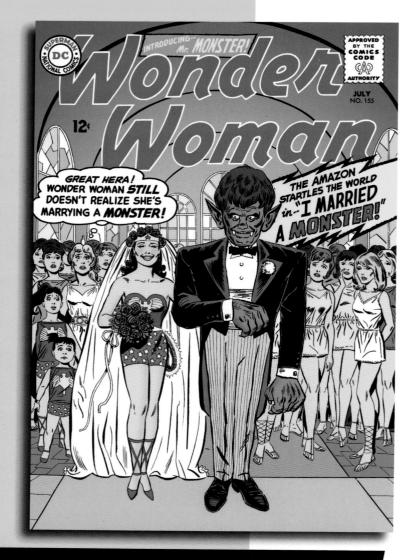

JULY 1965

MAIN CHARACTERS:
Wonder Woman • Mr. Monster

SUPPORTING CHARACTERS:
Hippolyta • Steve Trevor •
Wonder Girl • Wonder Tot •
Manno the Mer-Man •
Bird-Man

MAIN LOCATIONS:
Paradise Island • Statue
of Liberty

WONDER WOMAN
(VOLUME 1)
#155

WATCH WITH HORROR AS WONDER WOMAN PREPARES TO MARRY A MONSTER!

Encapsulating the very essence of this era of Wonder Woman, the heroine repeatedly attempts to escape the unwanted affection of her many suitors. However, she finds herself falling in love with the one man who treats her with contempt and disdain.

1 When Steve Trevor forces an unwanted kiss on Wonder Woman while demanding that she marry him, the Amazon escapes into the air. However, as she flies her Invisible Jet, she is soon ambushed by another would-be suitor, Bird-Man. He finds his way into her jet and steals another unwanted kiss.

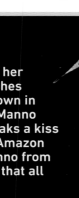

2 Tossing Bird-Man out of her plane, Wonder Woman crashes the jet into the sea. Deep down in the water, she encounters Manno the Mer-Man, who also sneaks a kiss from Wonder Woman. The Amazon Princess angrily ejects Manno from her plane, while lamenting that all men are the same.

3 Escaping back into the air, Wonder Woman witnesses an amazing sight—a spaceship castle crashing from the sky toward Paradise Island. Once the castle has safely landed, Wonder Woman investigates. She discovers that the singular inhabitant is a monstrous prince who wants nothing to do with the Amazon Princess or any other woman.

4 Brought to tears by this rejection, Wonder Woman vows to teach the prince that only his behavior matters, not his appearance. Confused and paranoid, the prince fires weapons upon the Amazon and her family. Impressed by his defiance and unconcerned with his appearance, she falls completely in love with him.

*"I **hate** you! I hate all women!"*

Mr. Monster

5 The prince is persuaded to marry Wonder Woman and despite the protests of Bird-Man and Manno, the ceremony begins. Before it can go too far, however, the prince flees, horrified that a beautiful girl would sacrifice happiness to be with a monster. Insistent on marrying the prince, Wonder Woman pursues him.

6 Outside, the pair are attacked by a sphinx. By acting nobly and heroically, the prince transforms, briefly becoming handsome. But despite Wonder Woman saving them both from the sphinx, the prince grows angry and ugly again. He storms off, leaving the Amazon Princess to wonder if she could make the prince love her if she learned to cook.

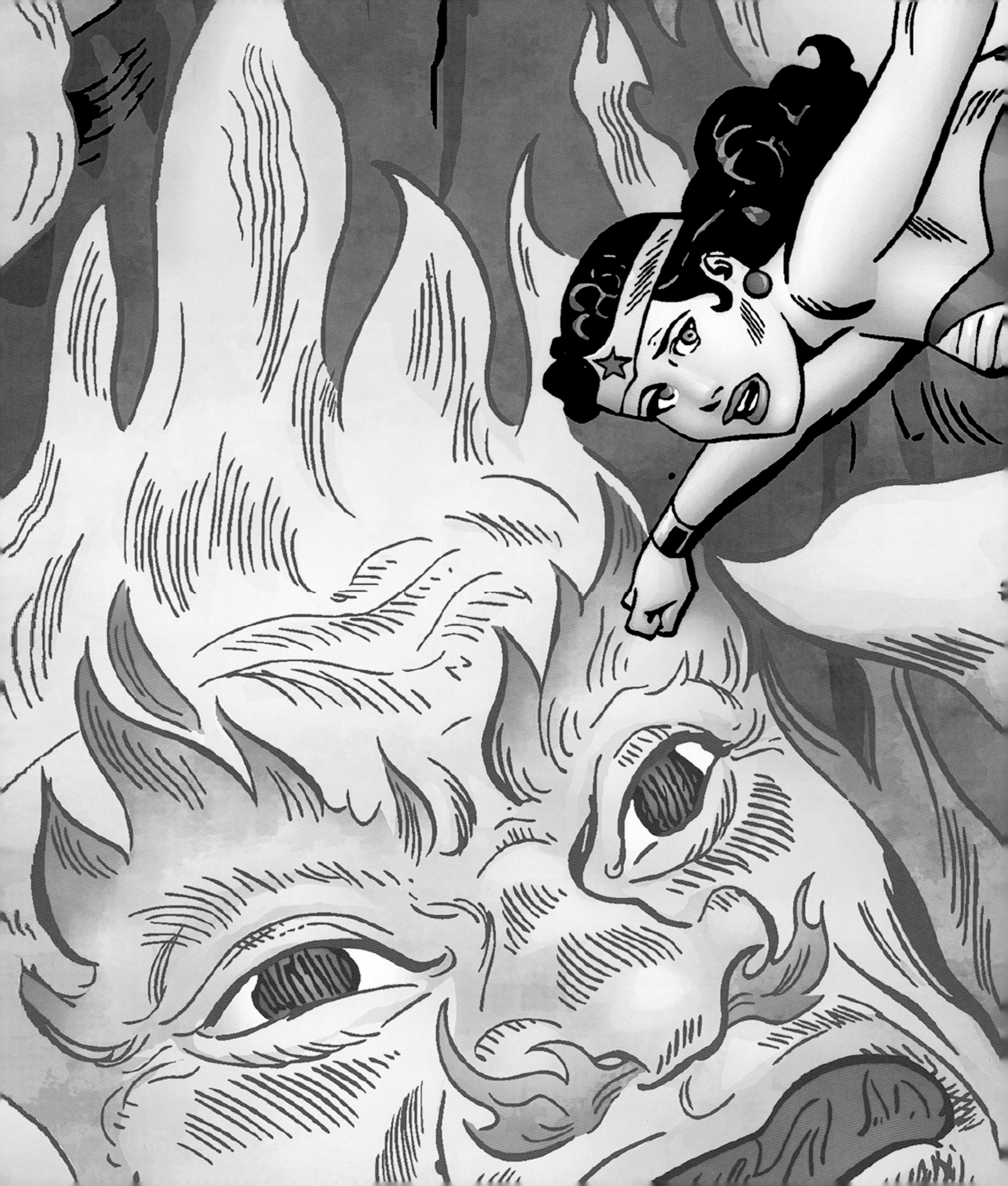

The rage of Aphrodite, the Goddess of Love, awakens a creature of fire that threatens to destroy Paradise Island.

Wonder Woman (Vol. 1) #149 (Oct. 1964)

JUSTICE LEAGUE OF AMERICA
(VOLUME 1)
#9

BANDED TOGETHER TO FIGHT THE EVILS OF THE WORLD, THEY ARE... THE JLA!

FEBRUARY 1962

The members of the Justice League of America retell the tale of their outrageous origin. Though not the first published story of the JLA, it is the first one to show the reader how it all began, and its influence would be felt for decades to come.

MAIN CHARACTERS:
Wonder Woman • The Flash • Green Lantern • Aquaman • The Martian Manhunter

SUPPORTING CHARACTERS:
Batman • Superman • Green Arrow • Snapper Carr • Amazons

MAIN LOCATIONS:
The planet Appellax • Earth

1 On the distant world of Appellax, a monstrous plan unfolds to conquer and enslave humanity. Leaderless, seven alien warlords from across Appellax conspire to use a distant planet as a battleground to decide their new ruler. Their plan is to transport themselves across the galaxy and mutate the indigenous people to form seven different armies.

2 Choosing Earth as the perfect place to stage their war games, the aliens are reduced in size and placed within meteors. Then, launched into space, each meteor is sent rocketing across the galaxy, each one targeting a different zone of humanity's remote world.

3 No force on Earth is powerful enough to withstand the combined might of these seven alien warlords. All those who resist would be transformed, their will subjugated, and their minds enslaved—all in the service of a cruel and menacing game of interstellar politics.

4 Though several of the competing warlords are defeated, one by one the Super Heroes of Earth fall victim to the most diabolical of the alien beings. It uses its power to transform the heroes into helpless tree creatures, rooted to the ground.

5 Undeterred by their apparent defeat, the collection of Super Heroes silently combines its efforts. With the help of her allies, Wonder Woman is transformed back to her human form, allowing her the strength she needs to battle the alien. The mighty Amazon is able to use her lasso to defeat the alien abomination.

"We're all helpless! How can we possibly **stop that creature?"**
MARTIAN MANHUNTER

6 Wonder Woman returns her newfound friends to their normal selves. Once the seven defeated warlords have been returned to their own planet, the assembled Super Heroes agree to create a league to fight for justice and protect humanity—and so the JLA, the Justice League of America, is founded.

THE JUSTICE LEAGUE

Through the course of her adventures, Wonder Woman meets countless allies and forms many friendships. None of those she encounters, however, prove to be as brave or as bold as the Super Heroes who band together to combat terrestrial or cosmic threats to Earth. Together, they are... The Justice League of America (JLA.)

THE ATOM

Scientist Ray Palmer discovered an alloy that gave him absolute control over his size and molecular density. Using this, he became the size-changing Super Hero known as the Atom.

AQUAMAN

Rightful King of Atlantis, Arthur Curry can breathe underwater and command marine life. He exhibits incredible strength and endurance.

LIGHT ATTACK

JLA foe Arthur Light prepares to use his invention, which will transport each of the Super Heroes to another dimension.

SUPERMAN

This strange visitor from another planet manages to be one of the most powerful and compassionate Super Heroes at the same time. Superman has sworn to use his powers to defend the helpless and battle evil.

THE MARTIAN MANHUNTER

The last living member of his species, the Martian Manhunter can transform his body in any way he imagines. His strength and speed almost match that of Wonder Woman.

BATMAN

Despite having no special powers, the Dark Knight's unparalleled skill in martial arts—as well as his high-tech, crime-fighting gear—make him a force to be reckoned with.

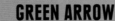

GREEN ARROW

Stranded for years on a deserted island, Oliver Queen survived by training himself to be an archer. When he returned to civilization, Oliver decided to use the skills he had gained to fight crime.

GREEN LANTERN

US Air Force pilot Hal Jordan was summoned by the dying alien Abin Sur to inherit the great power of the Green Lantern's ring. With it, he has become a member of an intergalactic corps of Super Heroes.

HAWKWOMAN

A police officer from the world of Thanagar, Shayera Thal came to Earth hunting a fugitive from her own world. Under the guise of Shiera Hall, she became a winged hero and member of the JLA.

THE FLASH

Struck by lightning while working in his crime lab, forensic scientist Barry Allen became the fastest man alive—and a founding member of the Justice League.

HAWKMAN

Katar Hol, Hawkwoman's husband and work partner, was the Imperial Prince of Thanagar before joining the police force. He came to Earth with his wife and joined the JLA as Hawkman.

BLACK CANARY

Driven by her mother's memories as a member of the Justice Society, Dinah Laurel Lance succeeded her as Black Canary. Armed with a sonic scream, she was a welcome addition to the Justice League.

WORLDS COLLIDE

Through the course of Wonder Woman's amazing adventures, it is inevitable that the Amazon would discover the existence of multiple realities, alternate Earths, and other incarnations of herself. Soon, the Wonder Woman of the Justice League of America would meet her Justice Society of America counterpart during the World War II era. But that is only the start...

A CRISIS ON TWO EARTHS

The Flash (Barry Allen) first paves the way for the heroes of Earth-One and Earth-Two to meet, his speed allowing him to bridge the gap between dimensions. Once he crosses to the other world, he finds his doppelgänger—the Flash of the Justice Society, Jay Garrick. They often pair up to face the foes of Earth-Two.

The Flash (Vol. 1) #129 (Jun. 1962) *Two Flashes from alternate dimensions take on two villains.*

INJUSTICE FOR ALL

With the heroes teaming up with alternate universe variations of themselves, it's unsurprising that the villains would do the same. A group calling themselves the Crime Champions—with teammates from both Earth-One and Earth-Two—soon attack the Justice League and the Justice Society. The combined forces of both teams are just enough to defeat the world-hopping super-villains.

JLA (Vol. 1) # 21 (Aug. 1963) *The Justice League and the Justice Society join together to defeat the Crime Champions.*

CRITICAL DIFFERENCES

Existing in two different divergent realities, the Wonder Woman of Earth-Two is decidedly older than the Wonder Woman of Earth-One, and eventually marries Steve Trevor. Their daughter, Hippolyta Trevor, succeeds Wonder Woman of Earth-Two as the Amazon's champion. She becomes the young hero known as Fury, a founding member of Infinity, Inc.

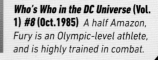

Who's Who in the DC Universe (Vol. 1) #8 (Oct.1985) *A half Amazon, Fury is an Olympic-level athlete, and is highly trained in combat.*

> "**Evil** isn't the reflection of **good**...
> **Good** is the reflection of **good**."
>
> WONDER WOMAN

Justice League of America (Vol. 1) #29 (Aug. 1964) Wonder Woman and other members of the JLA battle their Crime Syndicate counterparts.

THE CRIME SYNDICATE

Once the Justice League of America and the Justice Society of America become aware of their duplicate selves, meetings between the two worlds are common. Inevitably, the heroes of the two Earths gain the attention of their evil counterparts on Earth-Three, sinister villains seeking new souls to terrorize.

INFINITE ENEMIES

Even more deadly, this new cosmic-level battleground attracts cosmic-level threats. These include beings like Aquarius—who briefly banishes the entire universe of Earth-Two into a spirit realm, and the Anti-Matter Man—whose mere existence nearly causes Earth-One and Earth-Two to collide. The stakes for the heroes are rapidly growing higher as they test the boundaries of the impossibly vast Multiverse.

Wonder Woman (Vol. 1) #228 (Feb. 1977) Wonder Woman from Earth-One battles her Earth-Two counterpart.

Justice League of America (Vol. 1) #47 (Sep. 1966) Members of both the JLA and JSA battle the threat of the Anti-Matter Man.

MONSTROUS MENACES

As comic book publishing marches into the atomic era and the readership grows increasingly interested in science fiction, Wonder Woman's rogues shift from costumed war criminals into mutated monsters and alien invaders.

Y'GGPHU-SOGGOTH

While no one truly understands exactly what Y'ggphu-Soggoth is or where it came from, it is understood beyond a shadow of a doubt that this alien entity meant to unleash horror and destruction if given the chance. At one point, working with a government intent on America's destruction, the creature captured Steve Trevor and transformed him into a human bomb, launching Wonder Woman's boyfriend like an explosive missile. This nightmare being has returned on almost a dozen occasions, each time seemingly cracked into a thousand pieces and destroyed forever.

PAPER-MAN

A janitor named Horace Throstle fell into a vat of chemicals. Rather than being killed, Horace found his body had been transformed, and that he could now mimic the basic properties of paper. He soon became obsessed with Wonder Woman, and committed multiple crimes in the misguided belief this activity would impress her. Paper-Man was mistaken.

MULTIPLE MAN

Multiple Man came into existence within the heart of a nuclear explosion, and was seemingly indestructible. This villain could transform into whatever he desired, be it a cyclone, an iceberg, or an atomic missile. Over time, this sentient force of evil had learned to articulate his thoughts, as evidenced when he told Wonder Woman that he would destroy the Amazons and reduce Earth to a plaything.

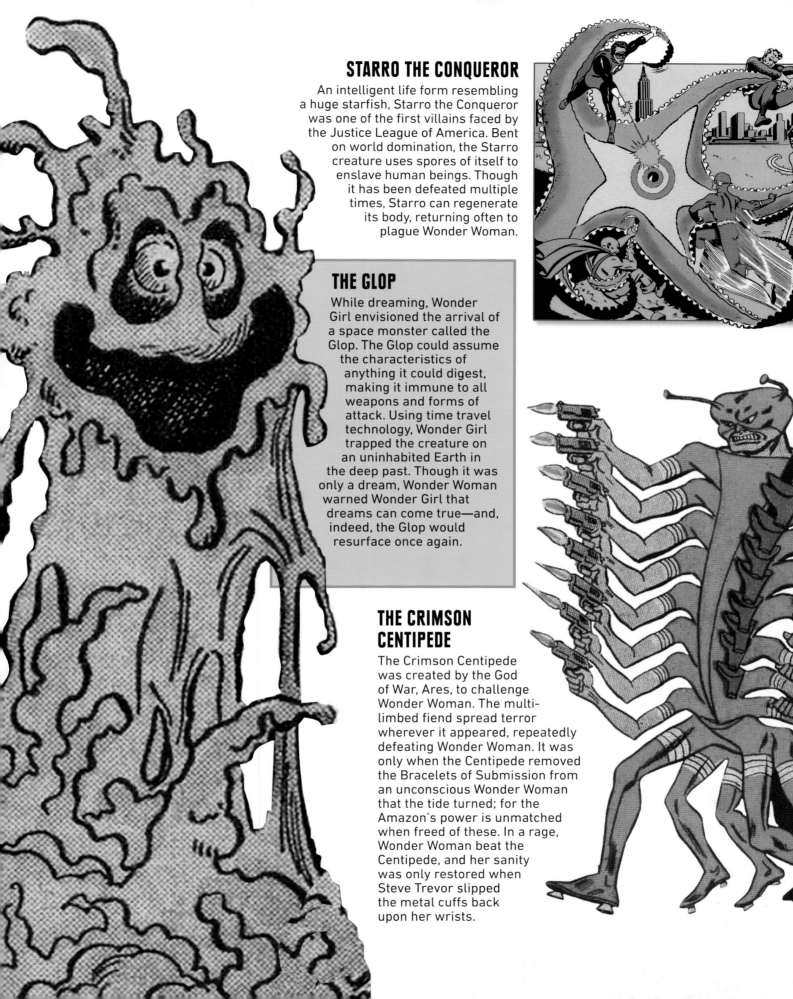

STARRO THE CONQUEROR

An intelligent life form resembling a huge starfish, Starro the Conqueror was one of the first villains faced by the Justice League of America. Bent on world domination, the Starro creature uses spores of itself to enslave human beings. Though it has been defeated multiple times, Starro can regenerate its body, returning often to plague Wonder Woman.

THE GLOP

While dreaming, Wonder Girl envisioned the arrival of a space monster called the Glop. The Glop could assume the characteristics of anything it could digest, making it immune to all weapons and forms of attack. Using time travel technology, Wonder Girl trapped the creature on an uninhabited Earth in the deep past. Though it was only a dream, Wonder Woman warned Wonder Girl that dreams can come true—and, indeed, the Glop would resurface once again.

THE CRIMSON CENTIPEDE

The Crimson Centipede was created by the God of War, Ares, to challenge Wonder Woman. The multi-limbed fiend spread terror wherever it appeared, repeatedly defeating Wonder Woman. It was only when the Centipede removed the Bracelets of Submission from an unconscious Wonder Woman that the tide turned; for the Amazon's power is unmatched when freed of these. In a rage, Wonder Woman beat the Centipede, and her sanity was only restored when Steve Trevor slipped the metal cuffs back upon her wrists.

IMPOSSIBLE TALES!

Wonder Woman appears in seemingly-impossible adventures together with her mother and two younger versions of herself. These "Impossible Tales" are thanks to a combination of Amazonian technology, dream sequences, and even a new Earth!

Wonder Woman (Vol. 1) #124 (Aug. 1961) *Thanks to clever film editing, the Wonder Family members can appear together.*

COMING OF AGE

As a teenager, Princess Diana of Paradise Island idolizes her older self, whose heroic activities she can view on the Amazons' "Time and Space Televisior." Before the teenager can receive her own costume, however, Diana must prove her worth. Hippolyta devises a series of challenges: a journey to the bottom of the sea, a trip into the heart of a volcano, and a climb to the top of a mountain.

Step into the Past

Hippolyta edits a recording made on the Time and Space Televisior. It creates the illusion that Princess Diana met and had adventures with herself as an adult, a teenager, and a toddler—Wonder Woman, Wonder Girl, and Wonder Tot—with each incarnation equally superpowered.

Wonder Woman (Vol. 1) #124 (Aug. 1961) *Diana and Hippolyta watch footage of Wonder Tot holding Wonder Woman aloft.*

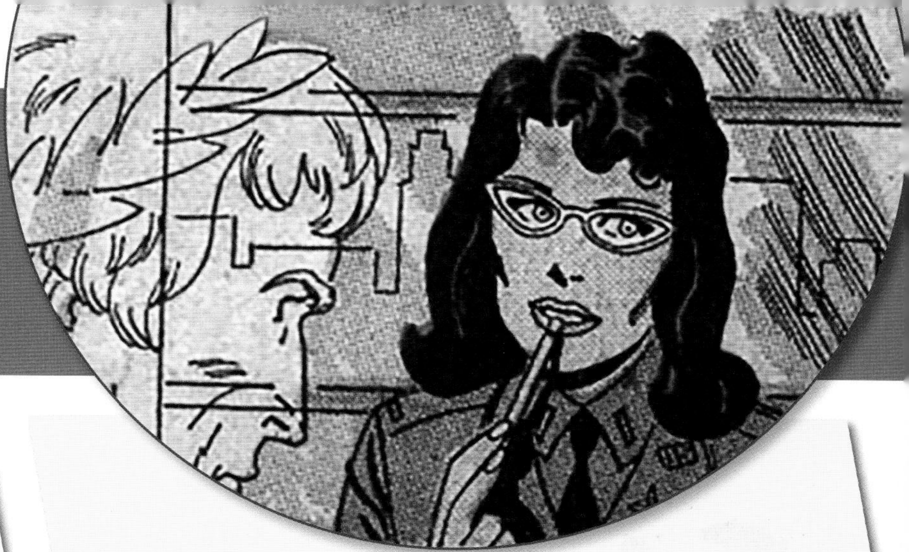

Wonder Woman (Vol. 1) #140 (Aug. 1963) *Morpheus appears to Diana at her workplace.*

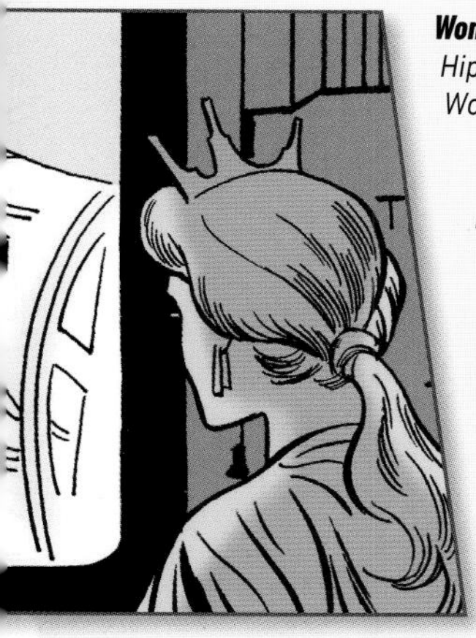

Wonder Woman (Vol. 1) #107 (Jul. 1959) *Hippolyta views a recording of Wonder Woman in her Invisible Jet.*

"It feels strange— ***watching myself*** *in this* ***time machine...***"

TEENAGED PRINCESS DIANA

WISH FULFILLMENT

When Wonder Woman is visited by Morpheus, God of Dreams, she is given the opportunity to choose three people for whom Morpheus will grant a wish. However, every wish causes trouble for each member of the Wonder Family. It turns out this entire "Impossible Tale" was all just a dream—a prank on Wonder Woman by the whimsical god of slumber.

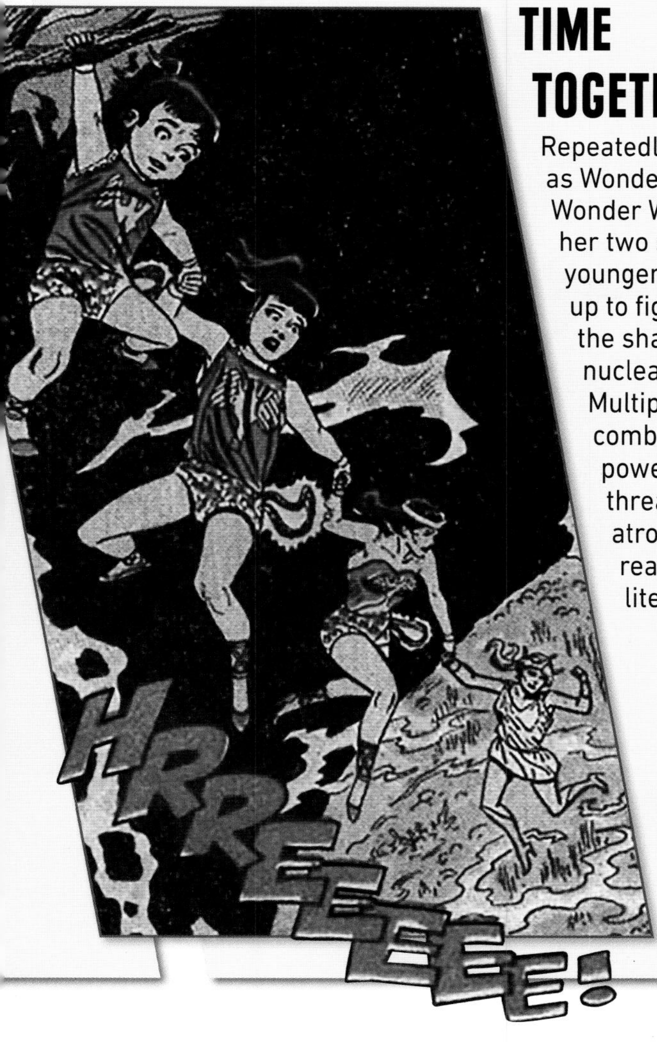
HRREEEEEE!

Wonder Woman (Vol. 1) #129 (Apr. 1962) *In a second "Impossible Tale," the Wonder Family again faces Multiple Man.*

TIME TOGETHER

Repeatedly Hippolyta—as Wonder Queen—Wonder Woman, and her two superpowered younger selves team up to fight villains like the shape-changing, nuclear-powered Multiple Man. They combine their great power to stop the threat of this atomic atrocity that can rearrange itself into literally anything!

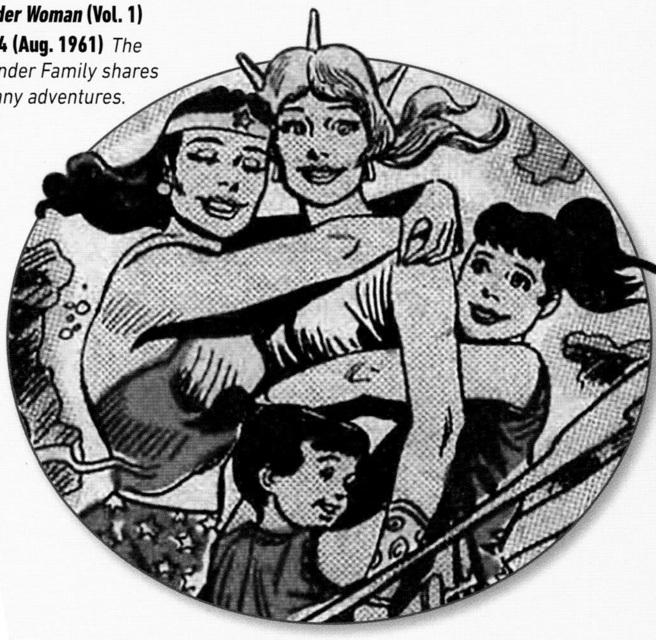

Wonder Woman (Vol. 1) #124 (Aug. 1961) *The Wonder Family shares many adventures.*

A Family United

Over and over again, the Wonder Family is united against a common enemy, all enjoying adventures together in an often inexplicable way. Eventually, during a cosmic crisis, these tales are erased from Wonder Woman's timeline—removed to their own reality in a parallel world called Earth-124.1, where the Wonder Family can live happily ever after.

With women's liberation coming to the fore, Wonder Woman shrugged off the shackles of her past and began a journey of empowerment and self-discovery. It was a rough road—the Amazon found how much she had yet to learn about being a role model and about the battle for equal rights!

THE BRONZE AGE

**Wonder Woman (Vol. 1) #179
(Nov.–Dec. 1968)**
The Amazon Princess must relinquish her powers to stay on Earth.

Wonder Woman (Vol. 1) #269 (Jul. 1980)
Wonder Woman quits in despair... and returns to Paradise Island.

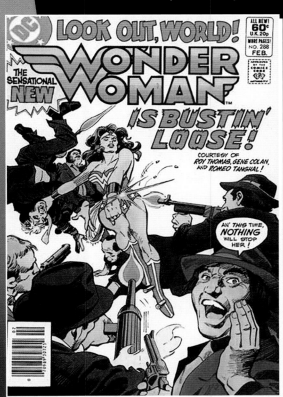

**Wonder Woman (Vol. 1) #288
(Feb. 1982)**
A new WW emblem is featured on Wonder Woman's costume.

LESSONS

If there is one thing Wonder Woman would realize during this Bronze Age, it is that she has a lot to learn. Whether being tested on her views of equality, training to become a Super Hero without powers, or rediscovering her place in the JLA, the lessons she learns are invaluable.

NEVER POWERLESS

Having forsaken her powers, Diana Prince—a Wonder Woman no longer—must retrain both her body and mind if she is to have any hope of continuing her mission of heroism. To this end, she diligently studies multiple forms of martial arts, all while under the guidance of her mentor, I-Ching.

Wonder Woman (Vol. 1)
#179 (Nov.–Dec. 1968)

UNCOMFORTABLE TRUTHS

When Wonder Woman is blinded by the prejudices ingrained in her from a lifetime of advantages, it takes the harsh words of a close friend to open her eyes and teach her a lesson in understanding. Realizing that she must fight for all women, Diana puts aside an opportunity for a highly paid job in fashion to fight for women's rights.

Wonder Woman (Vol. 1)
#203 (Nov.–Dec. 1972)

IDENTITY CRISIS

Stripped of her memories of the months she spent powerless —and consequently doubting her worth and place among the world's greatest heroes—Wonder Woman declares herself unfit to serve in the Justice League. To prove to herself and the team that she is qualified to return, the Amazon tests herself with 12 tasks of heroism.

Wonder Woman (Vol. 1) #220
(Oct.–Nov. 1975)

TEST OF CHARACTER

Wonder Woman must again undergo the tournament to earn the right to be the Amazon's emissary to Man's World. But when her compassion costs her the victory, Wonder Woman defies the will of the gods and returns to the US, saving thousands from a nuclear weapon, and proving the mantle to be rightfully hers. By her actions, Diana learns that it is not just her title that makes her a Wonder Woman.

Wonder Woman (Vol. 1) #250 (Dec. 1978)

SELF CONTROL

When Ares conspires to become master of Earth, he arranges to discredit Wonder Woman and replace her with a champion of his own choosing. Manipulated by the Greek Gods into losing control of her berserker fury, Wonder Woman is handcuffed and marched through the prison. So long as her wrists are chained by men, the Amazon cannot access the great powers gifted to her, and must control the rampaging emotions boiling within her if she wants to hold on to any hope of escape. It is a test of Wonder Woman's patience and restraint while at her lowest point—as was intended by the Olympians who stand against the God of War. Their hope is to provide their champion with a lesson in humility and control, qualities that Wonder Woman must master if she hopes to defeat Ares.

Wonder Woman (Vol. 1) #260 (Oct. 1979)

DEPOWERED

It is a time of great change for Wonder Woman. A time when her very identity comes under assault. Will the now-depowered Amazon rise to the challenges of the future, or be dragged down by the ghosts of her past?

NEW START

As the Amazons choose to leave Earth for another dimension, Wonder Woman makes the difficult decision to remain on Earth. Powerless, and without her family, she stays to help an endangered and outcast Steve Trevor. She is Wonder Woman and princess no more, instead she is simply Diana Prince—a role that the former hero must now redefine.

Wonder Woman (Vol. 1) # 179 (Nov.–Dec. 1968) *Diana renounces her Wonder Woman powers.*

Wonder Woman (Vol. 1) # 187 (Mar.–Apr.1970) *Red-hot coals pour onto Doctor Cyber's face—scarring her forever.*

Fall of a Hero

Working in secret for General Darnell—resulting in him being called a traitor to his country—Steve Trevor undertakes a heroic effort to discover the terrifying truths of Doctor Cyber. Steve is captured during his investigation, and shot while trying to escape and warn Diana Prince.

Wonder Woman (Vol. 1) #180 (Jan.–Feb. 1969) *The mastermind behind Steve's murder is revealed!*

THE TRUE FACE OF EVIL

As Doctor Cyber prepares to use her earthquake machine to destroy Hong Kong, Diana Prince watches helplessly while her mentor, I-Ching, is shot by his own daughter, Lu Shan. It is the moment of triumph for Doctor Cyber—a victory that is ripped away when the vain criminal is horribly injured by a brazier full of burning coals. Diana escapes, rushing I-Ching to the hospital while a disfigured Doctor Cyber is dragged away by Lu Shan, vowing revenge against Diana.

Wonder Woman (Vol. 1) #189 (Jul.–Aug. 1970) *Diana Prince helps to defend I-Ching's people.*

Wonder Woman (Vol. 1) #188 (May–Jun. 1970) *Doctor Cyber reveals the full extent of her injuries.*

EXPOSED

Diana Prince and her friend Patrick McGuire travel into Hong Kong to find and deactivate Doctor Cyber's earthquake machines. In the process, they are captured by the vengeful Cyber, who reveals the depth of her disfigurements. Crazed and irrational, Doctor Cyber lashes out blindly in battle against the former Princess of the Amazons, and ultimately falls to her own apparent death.

Wonder Woman (Vol. 1) #204 (Jan.–Feb. 1973) *Diana Prince sobs as I-Ching dies in her arms.*

THE FINAL CUT

I-Ching is tragically murdered by a sniper. Diana goes after the killer but is knocked unconscious. Now an amnesiac, she returns to Paradise Island, and assumes the role of Wonder Woman once more.

"Karate... judo... kung-fu... whatever I need... I've got!"
DIANA PRINCE

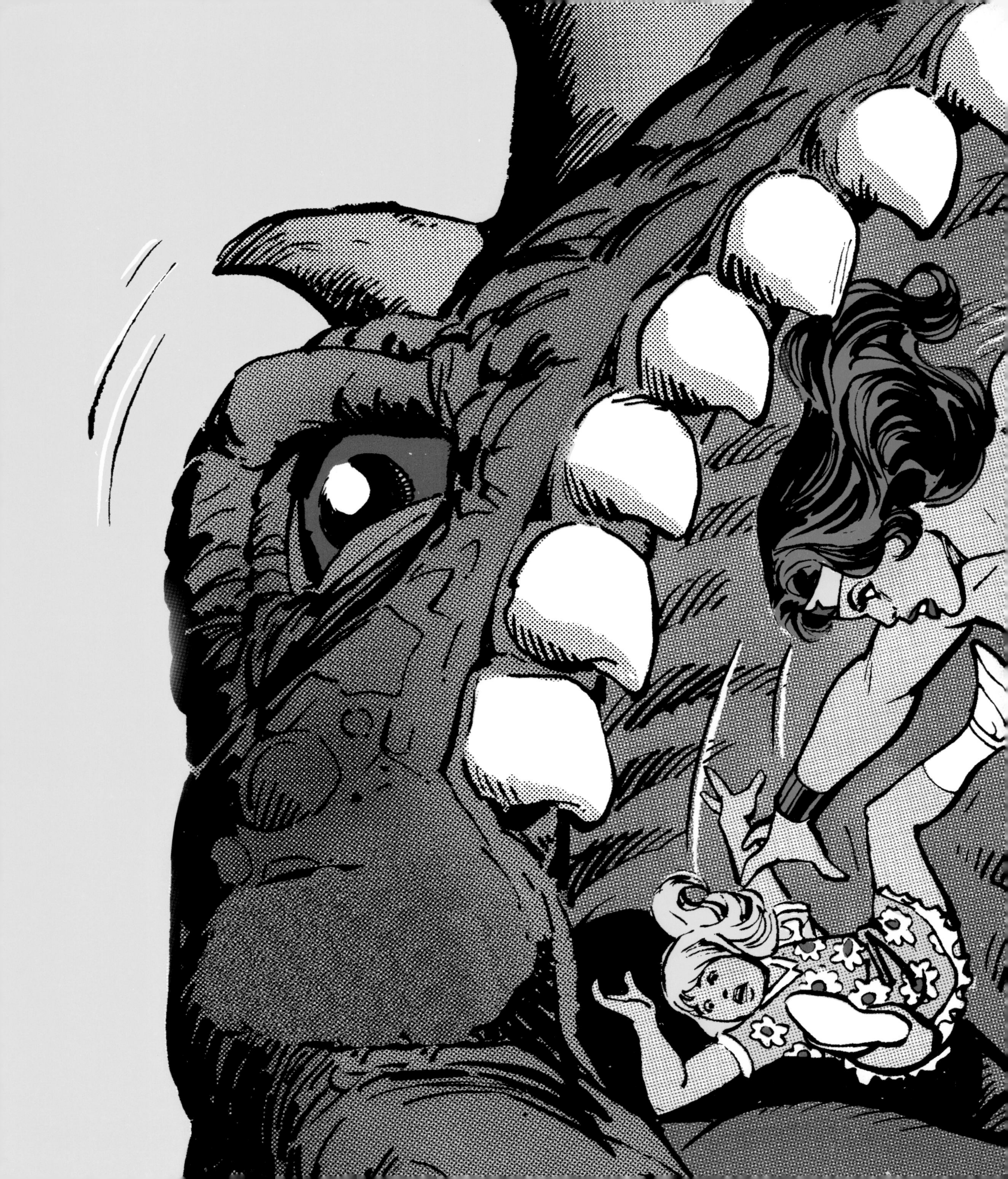

When a dinosaur inexplicably helps criminals rob an armored car, a young girl is endangered. Rather than let the child be eaten, Wonder Woman bravely throws herself into the creature's cavernous mouth.

Wonder Woman (Vol. 1) #257 (Jul. 1979)

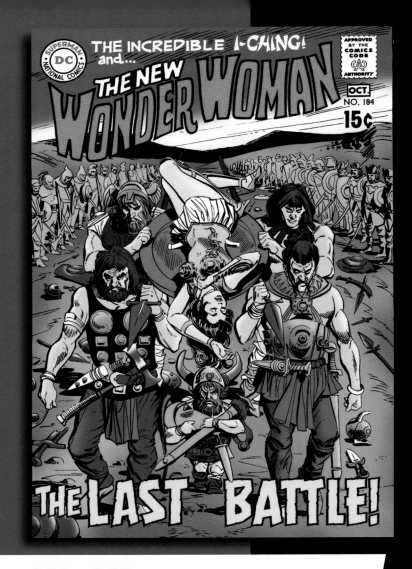

WONDER WOMAN
(VOLUME 1)
#184

THE EMISSARY OF PEACE MUST NOW BECOME THE SOLDIER OF WAR.

Comic book storylines were shifting to satisfy the readers' desire to see the complexities of life reflected in the struggles of their favorite heroes. This issue marks the beginning of Wonder Woman's gradual transformation from peacekeeping hero to sword-carrying warrior.

SEP.–OCT. 1969

MAIN CHARACTERS:
Wonder Woman • Ares • Hippolyta

SUPPORTING CHARACTERS:
Brunhilde • Drusilla • King Arthur and his court

MAIN LOCATIONS:
Paradise Island • Camelot

1 When the Amazons chose to temporarily abandon the dimension of Earth, Wonder Woman made the difficult choice to remain behind, sacrificing her powers in the process. Now she has been summoned to the new home of her people to lead the defense against the God of War, Ares, but with battle looming, her forces are badly outnumbered.

2 In a desperate bid to defeat Ares' oncoming horde, Wonder Woman plans to travel to the realm of the ancient heroes of Camelot. The Amazon leader commands her forces to retreat, and fight only when the odds suit them—anything they can do to stall and hold the line until she returns.

3 Unfortunately, Wonder Woman's pleas for help are ignored within the legendary court of Camelot. The heroes of old are tired and bitter, unwilling to continue fighting for the causes of others. Enraged at the hero Siegfried's caustic dismissal, Wonder Woman strikes him, initiating one-on-one combat.

4 Brunhilde, leader of the Valkyries, steps in to defend Wonder Woman. She swears her and her soldiers' allegiance to the Amazon hero as she does so. Brunhilde and her Valkyries return with Wonder Woman, arriving across the dimensional barrier just in time.

5 The tide of Ares' soldiers is too vast, overwhelming the Amazons despite the reinforcement of the Valkyries. Wonder Woman and her defenders are forced back until finally there is nowhere left to run. Then a thunder of hooves and a sound of horns herald the heroes of Camelot—the cavalry has arrived at last.

6 The battle is won, but at great cost. The hero Wonder Woman has fallen. Ares is touched at the valor his enemy has shown, and so carries her on a shield into the Amazon camp. He honors the unconscious Wonder Woman, but swears that he shall return.

*"There are **always** those who will follow."*

ARES

Hidden Depths

I-Ching's abilities extend far beyond the physical. The blind mentor is proficient in magic to some degree, a trait he rarely chooses to use or reveal. Regardless, his knowledge of the arcane is great enough that he was once able to thwart Morgana, daughter of the dreaded Morgan le Fey.

A Lost Childhood

Diana's mentor carries with him one half of a broken medallion, forever seeking the owner of the second half—his long lost daughter Lu Shan. Unfortunately, Lu Shan is in the employ of Doctor Cyber, and seeks revenge against I-Ching as she believes he was responsible for her mother's death when she was a child.

I-Ching usually carries a cane. He uses it as a weapon and a means to deceive others about his capabilities.

FIRST APPEARANCE: *Wonder Woman* (Vol. 1) #179 (Nov.–Dec. 1968)

OCCUPATION: Unknown

AFFILIATIONS: Unknown

POWERS/ABILITIES: Martial artist, mystic

ALTERNATES: Post-Crisis, I-Ching works with Batman and stands against Rā's al Ghūl.

THE PATH OF FATE

For as much as Wonder Woman would learn of I-Ching's origins, there is much about this father figure that has never been revealed to the Amazon. The shroud of mystery that surrounds I-Ching, ultimately, does not matter. Wonder Woman understands enough to know of her mentor's nobility and compassion in the face of adversity—lessons that are not ignored.

I-Ching typically wears a black suit. A skilled fighter, the stiff clothing does not slow him down.

ORIGIN

I-Ching is a mystical, blind man whose understanding and skill in the field of martial arts appears unparalleled. When the ancient monastery I-Ching studied in was raided by the forces of the villainous Doctor Cyber, fate brought him together with Diana Prince. The former Wonder Woman had just renounced her Amazon heritage and her Super Hero powers and the two quickly recognized each other as kindred spirits. I-Ching chose to train his new pupil in the arts of the ancient sect to which he once belonged. With both master and student dedicated to ending the evil of Doctor Cyber, Wonder Woman's life would be changed dramatically for the next few months of adventure.

"Fate has a long arm, Diana.
None can escape *its reach."*

I-CHING

Mystic of Steel

Once more tapping into his hidden mystic nature, I-Ching helps Superman project his astral self and search for clues about why his own powers are waning. It turns out that the Man of Steel's powers are being inadvertently absorbed by a being belonging to an alien race called the Quarrm. Recapturing Superman's lost abilities would risk an explosion that could shatter the world. Using some form of mystic skill, I-Ching is able to bring about a peaceful resolution, and the Quarrm alien returns to its formless existence.

I-CHING

Mysterious and mystical, the man known as I-Ching wanders into Wonder Woman's life and leaves it forever changed. Helping the Amazon learn through his wisdom and experience, he has shown her a very different world of heroics—based on martial arts and spiritual wisdom.

COLLEAGUES & FRIENDS

With the Amazons retreating to another dimension and Steve Trevor apparently dead, Wonder Woman suddenly finds her friendships in constant upheaval. As the civilian Diana Prince, she meets many people from all walks of life.

STACY MACKLIN

An astronaut trainee who worked alongside Diana Prince at NASA, Stacy was briefly possessed by the goddess Athena. Later, an accident with irradiated moonlight transformed Macklin into the super-villain Lady Lunar.

GENERAL PHILLIP DARNELL

A veteran pilot and former chief of military intelligence, General Phillip Darnell served as the head of special assignments for the Pentagon in Washington, D.C. It was here that he worked with both Steve Trevor and Diana Prince. When Steve was believed dead, the general pursued a romantic relationship with Wonder Woman. Rejected, he tried to start a relationship with Diana Prince instead.

PATRICK MCGUIRE

An associate of Diana's mentor I-Ching, Patrick McGuire accompanied Diana as she traveled to Hong Kong. Like most men who met the Amazon during this time, he was instantly enamored by her. McGuire managed to put this infatuation aside and help Diana fight the villainous Doctor Cyber. It was with McGuire and I-Ching's help that Diana defeated the criminal and ended her plan to destroy the city through an artificially induced earthquake.

JONNY DOUBLE

Jonny left a career in law enforcement to become a private investigator in San Francisco. He was hired by a publisher to recruit Wonder Woman as a bodyguard. She agreed, despite disapproving of the publisher's choice of material. Jonny moved to Manhattan to be closer to Diana, and was taken hostage by I-Ching's evil daughter, Lu Shan. Wonder Woman and Catwoman rescued Jonny, but a few weeks later, Diana was presumed dead, and Jonny returned to San Francisco broken-hearted.

RUSSELL ABERNATHY

Russell Abernathy was a former senator who rented an apartment to Diana and Etta Candy. During this time, Abernathy found himself the target of blackmail and engaged in several activities he later regretted, including allowing Etta Candy to be kidnapped. He suffered a debilitating heart attack shortly after.

CATHY PERKINS

After being hoodwinked into becoming a virtual slave for the sinister Top Hat and her gang, Cathy was given refuge by Wonder Woman. The teenage runaway soon became the depowered Amazon's roommate and employee, working at Diana's boutique until it closed. Later, she campaigned for the rights of women, which put Cathy at odds with her former employer when Diana failed to consider the gender pay gap.

KEITH GRIGGS

Major Keith Griggs was a former air-force officer who served alongside Steve Trevor and Diana Prince in General Darnell's special operations division. Griggs competed with Trevor for missions, and was often perceived as Darnell's favorite. When Diana Prince and Major Griggs were transported to South America, Griggs found himself romantically drawn to his colleague.

DATA FILE

FIRST APPEARANCE: *Brave and the Bold* (Vol. 1) #60 (Jun.–Jul. 1965)

OCCUPATION: Super Hero, photographer

AFFILIATIONS: Teen Titans, Amazons of Paradise Island

POWERS/ABILITIES: Super-strength, super-speed, flight

ALTERNATES: Later, every version of Donna is fused into one, and she becomes a guardian of the Multiverse.

ALTERNATE IDENTITIES

Though she began her career in crime-fighting as the little sister to the most powerful woman on Earth, Donna Troy has carved her own path across the landscape of Super Heroes. From her part in the original Teen Titans, to the role she eventually fills in the group of space police known as the Darkstars, Donna Troy saves countless lives and defeats numerous villains.

As part of a mission to assemble her costume, Wonder Girl found these adhesive stars in a clam.

Teen Titan

Donna assumed the mantle of Wonder Girl when she left the overly concerned eye of Queen Hippolyta on Paradise Island. She joined the newly formed Super Hero team, the Teen Titans. With Robin, Kid Flash, Aqualad, and Speedy, Wonder Girl battles out-of-this-world threats like the Mad Mod and the Separated Man.

The gold bird emblem on Wonder Girl's top is a clear nod to her mentor's original outfit.

Like all Amazons, Wonder Girl wears bulletproof bracelets.

ORIGIN

Orphaned as a toddler when her parents perished in a fire, Donna Troy was found by Wonder Woman and brought to Paradise Island. She was raised as Queen Hippolyta's daughter and Wonder Woman's younger sister. As she grew up—a mortal among immortals—Donna had difficulty adjusting, so was given powers to match those of her big sister via the Purple Ray—a device made by Wonder Woman.

*"I can do **anything** any boy can do—and **better!**"*

WONDER GIRL

Changing Styles

Over time, Donna discovers her own direction in the world beyond the Amazons and their island. It isn't long before she moves into her own apartment and changes her look—leaving behind the youthful copy of her mentor's costume in favor of one that is unique to her own growing identity.

Love and Friendship

Shortly after meeting, Donna started dating the Green Arrow's sidekick, Speedy. The relationship is on-again and off-again, with the lives of the two heroes never crossing paths for long enough to spark much else—despite being members on the same super team. Regardless, it is certainly enough to make some of her other infatuated teammates jealous.

WONDER GIRL: DONNA TROY

Young, bright, and powerful, Donna Troy blasts onto the scene as Wonder Woman's little sister, Wonder Girl. The titanic teen proves to embody everything Princess Diana represented as a Super Hero, all the while dedicating herself to serving a bold new generation.

SINISTER SCHEMERS

Having witnessed a real-life president resign in disgrace, comic book readers begin to see fewer fantasy and science fiction enemies. Instead, villains start to exhibit more realistic traits of deceit and corruption... in the extreme!

> *"Surely you know by now that Cyber is incapable of failure!"*
> — DOCTOR CYBER

KOBRA

An international terrorist who has battled many of Wonder Woman's colleagues, Kobra initiated attacks on the Amazon to stave off her investigation into his activities. In the process, he went so far as to create the second incarnation of Cheetah (Debbi Domaine). His ultimate plan was to destabilize the world by destroying the oil supply in the Middle East. It was derailed by Wonder Woman when she defeated his agents and reduced his headquarters to rubble.

THE PRIME PLANNER

The Prime Planner served the villain Kobra as the administrator of the Cartel, a death squad that deployed several super-assassins when needed. Wonder Woman allowed herself to be captured by the Cartel and the Prime Planner, attacking from within. Once she had defeated his operations, Wonder Woman unmasked the leader of the assassins. She was shocked to discover that the Prime Planner was a close associate of Diana Prince's—named Morgan Tracy—who worked for the UN's Crisis Bureau.

DOCTOR CYBER

Terrorist Doctor Cyber was a beautiful and determined woman, with a plan that involved holding the world hostage with the earthquake machines she had commissioned. In the process of confronting Wonder Woman, Doctor Cyber's face was badly burned by an urn of smoldering coal and she blamed Wonder Woman for her resulting disfigurement. Consequently, she donned a golden mask and superpowered exoskeleton that would allow her to battle her foe.

TEN OF SPADES

Mike Bailey was training alongside Diana Prince to be an astronaut for NASA, and—with Steve Trevor temporarily deceased—Diana began to have romantic feelings for the handsome gentleman. However, this all came crashing down when Wonder Woman unmasked the Ten of Spades, a member of the criminal Royal Flush Gang, and discovered Bailey's face staring back at her.

ANGLE MAN

"Angle" Andrews was a mobster who prided himself on always having a plan. This wasn't idle boasting either; the Angle Man constructed schemes that would likely have worked against an average mortal. Against Wonder Woman, he was clearly no match. Angle Man acquired a triangular machine from the planet Apokolips he called "the Angler," a device that could warp time and space. Unlike many of Wonder Woman's foes, Angle Man was rarely murderous, and seemed mostly interested in money.

ANTI-MONITOR

Coming from the anti-matter universe, the Anti-Monitor is the herald of death and destruction for all living things. In his quest to conquer all, he has annihilated thousands of realities from existence, and with each one, a billion lives. Given the opportunity, this creature of un-life would see all things erased and rewritten with anti-matter.

ORIGIN

Created the moment the Multiverse came into existence, the Anti-Monitor was one half of an avatar of research created by an infinite omniversal being known as the Overmonitor. The Anti-Monitor exists within pure anti-matter, and his twin—known as the Monitor— exists within the matter universe. Hungry to consume reality from the moment of his creation, the Anti-Monitor seeks the realities of the Multiverse and destroys them, growing stronger with each universe he consumes.

Death of Supergirl

Several heroes from the last five Earths gather together to assault the stronghold of the Anti-Monitor. The being's outer shell is destroyed by an enraged Supergirl, but the Kryptonian hero is struck down in turn by the anti-matter villain.

The Fate of the Flash

During the Crisis, a prisoner of the Anti-Monitor, the Flash (Barry Allen) uses his great speed to destroy the villain's anti-matter cannon. In doing so, he dramatically sets back the Anti-Monitor's plan to destroy the Earth of Wonder Woman and the Justice League. He is able to buy time for the heroes to rally their defense—an act that sadly costs the scarlet speedster his life.

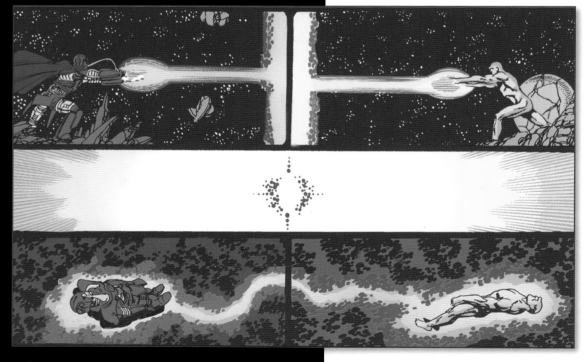

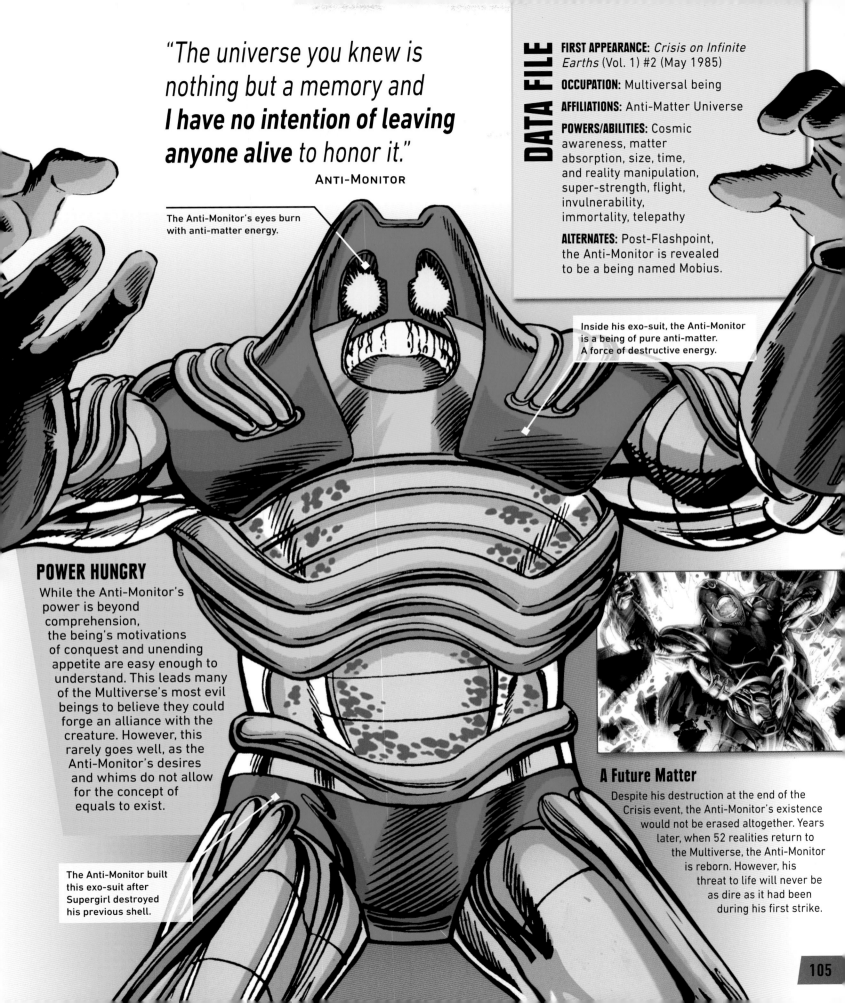

"The universe you knew is nothing but a memory and **I have no intention of leaving anyone alive** to honor it."

ANTI-MONITOR

The Anti-Monitor's eyes burn with anti-matter energy.

DATA FILE

FIRST APPEARANCE: *Crisis on Infinite Earths* (Vol. 1) #2 (May 1985)

OCCUPATION: Multiversal being

AFFILIATIONS: Anti-Matter Universe

POWERS/ABILITIES: Cosmic awareness, matter absorption, size, time, and reality manipulation, super-strength, flight, invulnerability, immortality, telepathy

ALTERNATES: Post-Flashpoint, the Anti-Monitor is revealed to be a being named Mobius.

Inside his exo-suit, the Anti-Monitor is a being of pure anti-matter. A force of destructive energy.

POWER HUNGRY

While the Anti-Monitor's power is beyond comprehension, the being's motivations of conquest and unending appetite are easy enough to understand. This leads many of the Multiverse's most evil beings to believe they could forge an alliance with the creature. However, this rarely goes well, as the Anti-Monitor's desires and whims do not allow for the concept of equals to exist.

The Anti-Monitor built this exo-suit after Supergirl destroyed his previous shell.

A Future Matter

Despite his destruction at the end of the Crisis event, the Anti-Monitor's existence would not be erased altogether. Years later, when 52 realities return to the Multiverse, the Anti-Monitor is reborn. However, his threat to life will never be as dire as it had been during his first strike.

DEATH OF WONDER WOMAN

All stories must come to an end, even those of the world's greatest heroes. It is Wonder Woman's finest moment as she helps lead her friends and allies into a cosmic war of epic proportions—but one that ultimately results in her death.

Crisis on Infinite Earths #9 (Dec. 1985) *Overwhelmed, Wonder Woman is struck by Eclipso.*

GATHERING OF FORCES

Though the cosmic villain known as the Anti-Monitor has consumed and erased many realities, the battle is stalled as Earth-One and Earth-Two seek refuge within a pocket universe, temporarily outside the reach of the enemy. Taking advantage of this respite, Wonder Woman and her allies band together to plan their attack against this evil, knowing full well that even in victory, many will fall.

Crisis on Infinite Earths #5 (Aug. 1985) *The heroes plan their next move.*

The Final Five

The entity named Harbinger uses the cosmic powers planted within her to draw three dying Earths away from the corrosive anti-matter of the enemy. There are now five surviving realities, each with its own version of Earth and its own heroes, ready to fight.

EVIL ATTACKS

The Anti-Monitor is seemingly defeated, and his plans have been derailed. But as five Earths have been left coexisting within the same time and space, the villains of the Multiverse band together to conquer and destroy their heroic counterparts forever. The heroes fall, one by one, under the assembled might of the villains, while the Anti-Monitor works in secret to wipe out history itself.

Crisis on Infinite Earths #6 (Sep. 1985) *Harbinger tries to save as many realities as she can.*

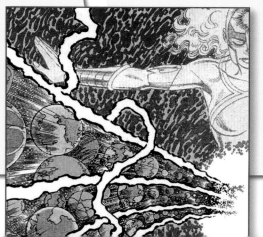

> "You will **die!** Then your world and very universe will follow you into **oblivion!**"
>
> ANTI-MONITOR

Crisis on Infinite Earths #12 (Mar. 1986) *The Anti-Monitor's blast catches Wonder Woman unprepared.*

Wonder Woman (Vol. 1) #329 (Feb. 1986) *Wonder Woman prepares to face the agents of the Anti-Monitor.*

THE FINAL STRIKE

The Anti-Monitor has returned, and been defeated once more. But the power that fuels this wretched force of darkness is not easily vanquished. As he falls, the Anti-Monitor manages one last, hate-filled strike. Wonder Woman is blasted back into the clay from which she was formed, erasing the existence of the most powerful woman to ever walk any world.

Enter the Dark Age...

In the end, the heroes manage to save only one world from the Anti-Monitor. It is a new world, one that is darker than its predecessors. It contains the core of the Multiverse, condensed into a singular reality. A reality that will soon include a new incarnation of Wonder Woman—a hero reborn, with an unwritten path stretching out before her.

Crisis on Infinite Earths #11 (Feb. 1986) *A New Earth lives on as the combination of five realities.*

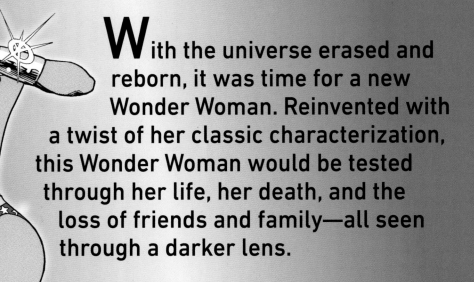

With the universe erased and reborn, it was time for a new Wonder Woman. Reinvented with a twist of her classic characterization, this Wonder Woman would be tested through her life, her death, and the loss of friends and family—all seen through a darker lens.

THE DARK AGE

Wonder Woman (Vol. 2) #20 (Sep. 1988)
Wonder Woman investigates the
tragic death of a friend.

Wonder Woman (Vol. 2) #57 (Aug. 1991)
Following a hotel massacre involving a group of
Amazons, Wonder Woman becomes a suspect.

Wonder Woman (Vol. 2) #126
(Oct. 1997)
Wonder Woman's life hangs in the
balance following a battle in Hell.

LOSS

In the Dark Age, the enemies and perils that Wonder Woman faces seem to grow increasingly deadly. It is inevitable that during this era of ever-escalating violence and danger, there are casualties in the never-ending battle against the forces of evil.

DEATH OF A FRIEND

Myndi Mayer was a highly driven publicist, whose vision to market Wonder Woman through an aggressive media campaign helped Diana quickly spread the Amazon message of peace and harmony. Unfortunately, Myndi does not live to see the fruits of her labor. This is Diana's first loss as a hero, and one for which she cannot help but blame herself.

Wonder Woman (Vol. 2) #20 (Sep. 1988)

HOMELESS AND HELPLESS

With the mysterious vanishing of Themyscira and its inhabitants, Wonder Woman has lost her home and her family. Homeless and broke, she resorts to sleeping on a friend's couch in the basement. Unable to bring herself to use her skills as a Super Hero to earn money, Diana forges onward as best she can, eventually taking a minimum wage job in a fast-food restaurant to make ends meet.

Wonder Woman (Vol. 2) #73 (Apr. 1993)

ORPHANED

The sorceress Circe constructs a plan to destroy Wonder Woman, piece by piece. Her first step is the most brutal, to kill Queen Hippolyta and destroy Themyscira, all while magically allowing Wonder Woman to helplessly witness the murderous attack. In the end it is revealed that the death of the Amazon is just a trick. But for Wonder Woman, the loss feels all too real.

Wonder Woman (Vol. 2) #76 (Jul. 1993)

BROKEN SPIRIT

After falling in battle against the dark demon Neron, Wonder Woman's soul is believed to have been destroyed, leaving her living body an empty shell. Diana's Justice League teammates visit their lost colleague, each trying one after another to use their great powers to reach her suffering spirit. One by one, the heroes fail. Together they try again, attempting to bring Diana back from the abyss. Once more they fail, and a great light is one step closer to being lost forever to the world.

Wonder Woman (Vol. 2) #125
(Sep. 1997)

GODS AND MORTALS

Having won her right to fulfill the mission of the Olympian Gods and travel beyond the shores of Themyscira, Princess Diana soon faces the first and greatest challenge of her life—battling against a mad and powerful god, bent on total destruction.

Coming to America

Having vanquished Ares' agent and stopped the bomb from destroying her island home, Wonder Woman is guided by Hermes to Boston, Massachusetts, in the USA. There, she delivers the wounded Steve to a hospital and seeks an ally to help her unravel the mysterious plan of war that is brewing.

Wonder Woman (Vol. 2) #3 (Apr. 1987) With Hermes at her side, Wonder Woman arrives in Boston, Massachusetts.

BOMB ON BOARD

When one of Ares' human agents attempts to drop a bomb on the island of the Amazons, Wonder Woman encounters Steve Trevor for the first time. Hijacked, and unaware of his co-pilot's sinister motivation, the colonel struggles to stop the possessed human—but he is too late.

Wonder Woman (Vol. 2) #2 (Mar. 1987) Consumed by Ares' power, Steve's co-pilot attempts to kill him and drop a bomb on Themyscira.

THE TOUCH OF DEATH FROM DECAY

Determined to stop the Amazon Princess in her mission to spread peace, the children of Ares—Deimos and Phobos—bring to life the being known as Decay. They send out the vile creature to inflict chaos and terror on the people that Wonder Woman has come to know. Wonder Woman defeats Decay, but not before her new friend, young Vanessa Kapatelis, is injured.

Wonder Woman (Vol. 2) #4 (May 1987) As the Kapatelis' house is destroyed by Decay, Wonder Woman flees with Julia and her daughter, Vanessa.

> *"By the powers the Gods have granted me, I shall not fail!"*
> WONDER WOMAN

Wonder Woman (Vol. 2) #5 (Jun. 1987) Wonder Woman realizes Ares plans to destroy Earth by coercing his followers into capturing an American nuclear missile base.

THE ASSAULT OF ARES

Having escaped an assassination attempt at the hospital, Steve Trevor, with the help of Etta Candy, investigates the strange events they have witnessed. This leads them to the home of Julia Kapatelis, and the location of Wonder Woman. Together, the group is able to discover the truth of Ares' plot—nuclear Armageddon and the end of all mortal life on Earth.

Wonder Woman (Vol. 2) #1 (Feb. 1987) Diana, Amazon Princess, prepares to take on the might of Ares, God of War.

Wonder Woman (Vol. 2) #6 (Jul. 1987) Physically superior, the god Ares dominates the battle with Wonder Woman... for a time.

POWER AT PLAY

While Steve Trevor and the others fight the possessed human forces of Ares, Wonder Woman finds herself battling the God of War himself. It is not a fight the Amazon has a hope of winning. Not directly. But when she uses the Golden Lasso of Truth to prove to Ares that his plan will result in his own ruin, the mad god finally relents, declaring that he will no longer attempt to incite such destruction on the world.

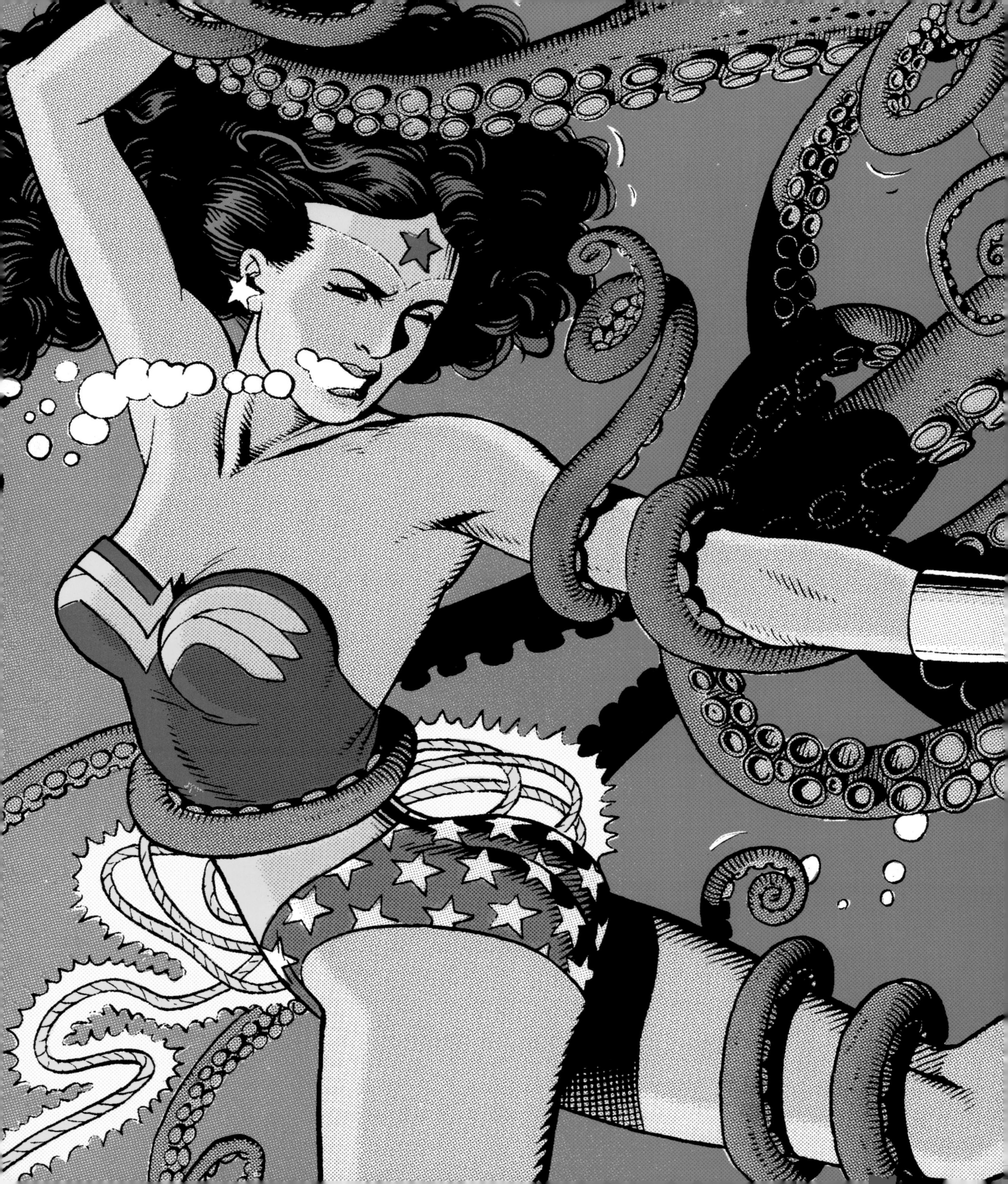

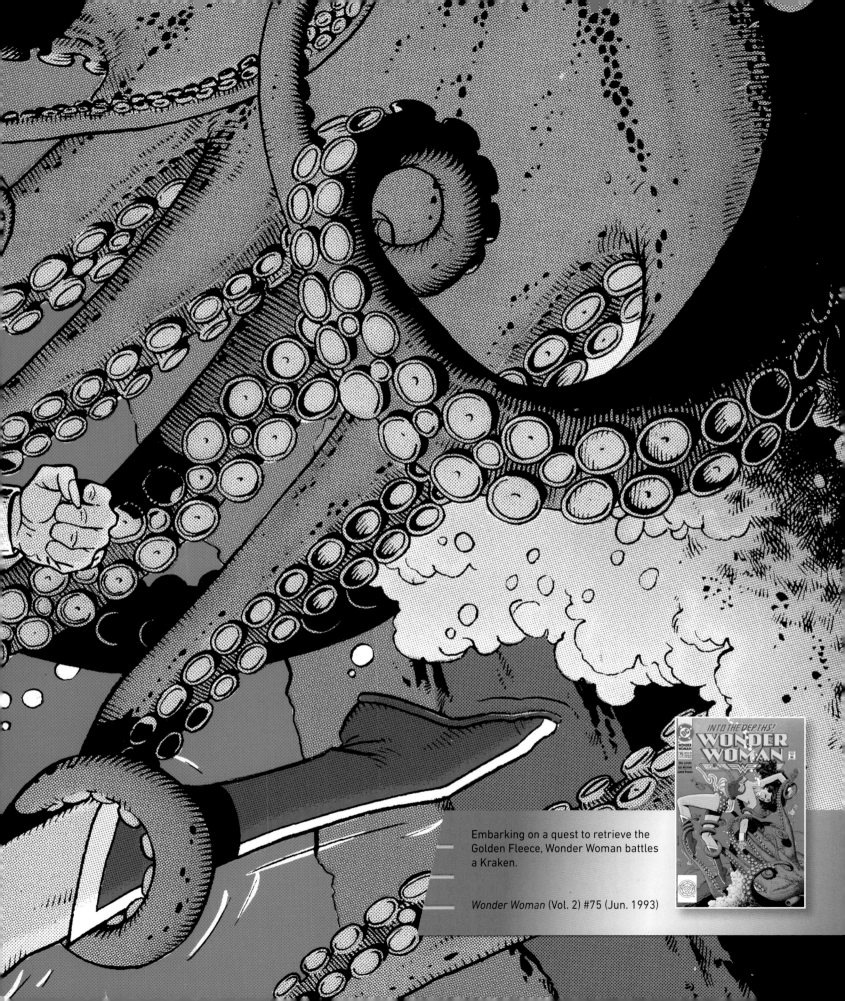

Embarking on a quest to retrieve the Golden Fleece, Wonder Woman battles a Kraken.

Wonder Woman (Vol. 2) #75 (Jun. 1993)

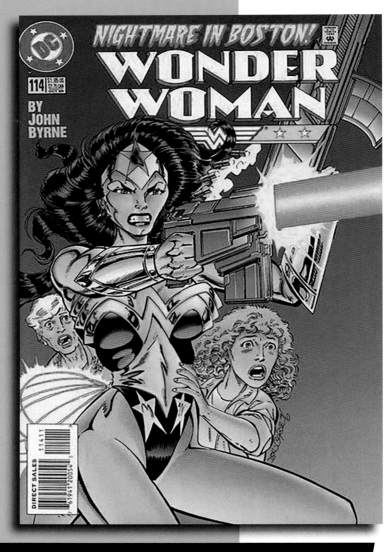

OCTOBER 1996

WONDER WOMAN
(VOLUME 2)
#114

AN INNOCENT MIND IS CORRUPTED THROUGH A VOLLEY OF NIGHTMARES.

The villain known as Doctor Psycho has begun to torture the mind of young Vanessa Kapatelis, a friend of Wonder Woman's. This is the start of Vanessa's transformation from happy teenager to brainwashed and cybernetically enhanced super-villain.

MAIN CHARACTERS:
Vanessa Kapatelis • Doctor Psycho

SUPPORTING CHARACTERS:
Wonder Woman (dream)

MAIN LOCATION:
Boston

1 Waking up in her bed, screaming after a particularly brutal nightmare, Wonder Woman's young friend Vanessa makes her way toward the sink to wash her face. As she stares into the mirror, her skin begins to melt away and her arms become liquid. She dissolves into the sink and swirls down into the drain, screaming as she goes.

2 Vanessa wakes up screaming once more, startled from her nightmare. Troubled by the frequency and intensity of her bad dreams, the teen stumbles across the carpet, unaware that the spiral pattern on the rug is actually a hungry maw, gaping wide enough to swallow her whole.

3 Vanessa's friend Wonder Woman arrives on the scene, saving her in the nick of time. But when Vanessa questions the coincidence of Wonder Woman's arrival, the Amazon goes berserk and attempts to murder Vanessa herself! She grabs the girl and smashes her face through a wall, then drops her into a pit of fire.

> *"Illusion so real it can kill."*
> **DOCTOR PSYCHO**

4 Meanwhile, at a psychological institute nearby, the inmate known as Doctor Psycho prepares to use his mind-bending powers to torture the unsuspecting physicians. Then, musing over his casual torment of Vanessa, he makes a bold escape.

5 Certain that she has finally awoken to a true reality, Vanessa runs through her home seeking her mother, Julia. But when she finds her mother transforming into a demon, it is up to Wonder Woman again to save her—this time while wielding a pair of blasters.

6 Wonder Woman blasts the demonic Julia, deciding next to end the life of Vanessa. Knowing that she is dreaming, but also aware that there is a power behind the dreams, Vanessa wills Wonder Woman to become her friend again. In doing so, she finally frees herself from the never-ending nightmare … for now.

ENTER ARTEMIS

When Hippolyta is plagued with visions of Wonder Woman's death, she announces there will be a contest to find a replacement for her daughter as emissary to Man's World. This is a desperate move from a mother wishing to shield her own daughter.

*"I have **accomplished more** here in four months than you have in four years!"*
— ARTEMIS

Wonder Woman (Vol. 2) #90 (Sep. 1994) *Diana of Themyscira argues with fellow Amazon Artemis of Bana-Mighdall before they fight for the title of Wonder Woman.*

AMAZON RIVALS

Manipulated into a contest of champions, tensions rise between Princess Diana and the rebellious Amazon of the Bana-Mighdall tribe, known as Artemis. Though Artemis believes she has no chance of winning what she thinks is a contest rigged against her and her tribe, Wonder Woman falters in the end... and loses out to her rival.

Wonder Woman (Vol. 2) #98 (Jun. 1995) *Artemis attacks Diana, calling her a traitor.*

A New Wonder Woman

Having surprised the Amazons by winning the challenge, Artemis is granted powers through a strength-enhancing gauntlet and winged shoes. She can now take on her new role as Wonder Woman. Unwilling to give up her life as a Super Hero, Princess Diana dons a new uniform and continues to battle evil and corruption in the world of men.

Wonder Woman (Vol. 2) #93 (Jan. 1995) *With the archer Artemis wearing the Wonder Woman costume, Diana adopts a new black outfit.*

Wonder Woman (Vol. 2) #100 (Jul. 1995) Artemis faces the White Magician in his demonic form.

DECEPTION

Convinced that Wonder Woman has betrayed her, Artemis attacks the Amazon Princess. In truth, Artemis has been manipulated by a villain known as the White Magician, who has been hiring actors to attack the fledgling Super Hero. Unaware of the extent to which she has been deceived, Artemis is convinced that Diana is trying to undermine her authority as Wonder Woman.

FINAL BATTLE

Realizing that Hippolyta has been harboring a secret that lies at the heart of Artemis' elevation to the role of Wonder Woman, Diana returns to Themyscira. Meanwhile, Artemis, now aware that she has been manipulated by a dark villain, faces the demonic White Magician on her own.

FALL OF AN AMAZON

Diana is magically transported to Artemis' side. Although she defeats the White Magician, she is too late. Artemis has fallen. With her dying breath, the Amazon of Bana-Mighdall relinquishes the mantle of Wonder Woman. She bestows it on Diana, recognizing that her own arrogance and ambition have been her downfall, and that there is only one true Wonder Woman—Princess Diana.

Wonder Woman (Vol. 2) #100 (Jul. 1995) Wearing Artemis' Gauntlets of Atlas, Diana is victorious.

Wonder Woman (Vol. 2) #98 (Jun. 1995) Artemis demands that Diana leave the city, falsely believing that her Amazon sister has been spreading lies about her.

WONDER GIRL: CASSIE SANDSMARK

The second teenage sidekick to the amazing Amazon, Cassie Sandsmark has gone to great lengths and feats of incredible bravery to prove that she is a true hero. She has battled alongside Wonder Woman, showing the world that she is more than ready for the title of Wonder Girl.

ORIGIN

When Diana came to Gateway City and visited Professor Helena Sandsmark in search of a job and a place to stay, 14-year-old Cassie—the archaeologist's daughter—was overjoyed. Unbeknown to Wonder Woman, Cassie snuck into the Amazon's room and "borrowed" the Sandals of Hermes and Gauntlets of Atlas. Donning a black wig and goggles to hide her identity, Cassie turned up to try to help Wonder Woman take down a clone of Doomsday, but was instantly ordered to leave. Undeterred, Cassie went on to fight the wandering spirit of Decay. Despite her acts of courage, Cassie's mother forbade the fledgling Wonder Girl from continuing her acts of heroism. Soon after, Cassie found herself in the realm of Olympus, and asked Zeus directly for the powers needed to become Wonder Girl. Admiring Cassie's courage, he agreed.

"Call me... Wonder Girl!"
CASSIE SANDSMARK

Young Justice

At a time when Cassie was still struggling with her role as a Super Hero, she joined the heavily mentored team of super teens called Young Justice. There, she worked and trained with several other junior Super Heroes, including Superboy, Impulse, Arrowette, and Miss Martian. Eventually, she even became team leader, beating out the third incarnation of Robin for the role.

Teen Titans

After Cassie's friend and predecessor in the role of Wonder Girl, Donna Troy, is killed by an out-of-control android, Cassie is devastated. She feels that her team has failed, and consequently leads the move to disband Young Justice. In the months that follow, circumstances lead to Cassie and several team members regrouping and resurrecting the name of Teen Titans.

Forged by Amazons, Cassie's bracelets can block almost anything.

Unlike Wonder Woman or Donna Troy, Wonder Girl's magical lasso channels the fury and lightning power of Ares, the God of War.

Of all the Teen Titans, Cassie changes her look regularly.

DATA FILE

FIRST APPEARANCE: *Wonder Woman* (Vol. 2) #105 (Jan. 1996)

OCCUPATION: Super Hero

AFFILIATIONS: Young Justice, Teen Titans, Amazons of Themyscira, Olympian Gods

POWERS/ABILITIES: Super-strength, super-speed, invulnerability, flight

ALTERNATES: In an alternate reality, Cassie Sandsmark and Donna Troy are the same age and compete for the right to be Wonder Girl.

Super Romance

Cassie was romantically involved with Superboy, right up until the young Kryptonian clone's death in her arms. Cassie was long in recovering from this loss, particularly as Wonder Woman vanished for a year shortly after. Though she felt angry and abandoned, Cassie eventually found peace.

LIKE FATHER, LIKE DAUGHTER...

Fun-loving and happy-go-lucky one moment, then stern and self-righteous moments later, Cassie Sandsmark ranges the gambit of emotions, often wearing her feelings on her sleeve for all to see. In this manner, she is very much like Zeus, the God of Lightning and Lord of Olympus, who is not only Cassie's benefactor, but also secretly her father.

SOCIAL CIRCLE

With the Crisis event having erased Wonder Woman's long history, the Amazon finds herself forging new friendships and romantic entanglements. In this reality, she meets most of her friends through scholarly circles and crime-fighting.

JULIA KAPATELIS

Julia was the Dean of History and Geology at Harvard University. As a child, Julia fell from a boat and was rescued by Poseidon, who placed her on Themyscira. Julia's memories were erased and she was returned to her family, subconsciously carrying the Amazons' message of peace and equality. Years later, Julia was chosen to mentor Wonder Woman in the ways of the patriarchal world.

HELENA SANDSMARK

Helena was the curator of the Gateway City Museum of Antiquities and a former pupil of Harvard professor Julia Kapatelis. Helena became a mentor and friend to Wonder Woman when the Amazon Princess moved to Gateway City, as did Helena's teenage daughter, Cassie. When young Cassie became Wonder Girl, Helena hesitantly gave her approval, provided that Cassie receive the proper training needed to care for herself. Helena endured her misgivings as best she could—supporting her daughter's heroic endeavors to the point where she helped supervise Cassie's time with teen super team, Young Justice.

VANESSA KAPATELIS

A high school student who befriended Wonder Woman, Vanessa dreamed of fighting evil alongside the Amazon Princess. When it became clear that this fantasy would never materialize, the young girl's adoration twisted into jealousy and anger, manipulated by several of Wonder Woman's enemies, including the enchantress Circe. These foes used psychological conditioning and cybernetic implants to turn Vanessa into the third villain to use the name Silver Swan.

MYNDI MAYER

Myndi Mayer situated herself into Wonder Woman's life soon after the Amazon's arrival from Paradise Island. As a publicist, she helped Wonder Woman deliver her message of peace and develop her brand identity of heroism. Much of Myndi's fast-talking bravado was an act designed to cover up considerable suffering. This ultimately led to her tragic death by a suspected overdose.

INSPECTOR INDELICATO

A police inspector and aspiring novelist, Ed Indelicato forged a friendship with Wonder Woman while investigating the apparent murder of publicist Myndi Mayer. Indelicato admired Wonder Woman, even risking his career in the police force to stand by the Amazon. A budding writer, Indelicato wrote two books about his adventures alongside Wonder Woman. The manuscript of Indelicato's first book was lost in a fire, but his second volume became a bestseller.

MIKE SCHORR

Mike Schorr was a member of the Gateway City police force, who traveled to the planet Apokolips with Wonder Woman and faced down Darkseid. He later accompanied the Amazon known as Artemis into the fiery depths of Hell to rescue Helena Sandsmark from the sorceress Morgan le Fey. Over time, Schorr developed romantic feelings for Wonder Woman, and was heartbroken and bitter when they were not requited. Eventually, the two friends drifted apart.

JASON BLOOD

Secretly the human half of the ancient demon known as Etrigan, Jason Blood used his arcane knowledge and centuries of experience to help protect the world against mystical threats. He briefly entered into a relationship with Helena Sandsmark, one that was unable to endure the demon's curse.

123

A NEW GOLDEN AGE

After Wonder Woman falls in battle against the demon Neron, Hippolyta rushes to her side, but is too late to save her weakened daughter. As the Gods make Diana the Goddess of Truth, Hippolyta becomes the new Wonder Woman.

PAST IMPERFECT

Early on in her new role as Wonder Woman, Hippolyta is approached by the original Flash—Jay Garrick—who has mysterious memories of Hippolyta as Wonder Woman during World War II. The pair travel back in time to the days of the Justice Society of America, and though there is some initial confusion and conflict between the future teammates, Hippolyta chooses to remain for eight years and fight alongside the JSA.

JSA (Vol. 1) #4 (Nov. 1999) The new JSA gathers at the dawn of the 21st century.

Wonder Woman (Vol. 2) #131 (Mar. 1998) Hippolyta meets Hawkman for the first time.

Like Mother, Like Daughter

After Diana has returned to the world and assumed the role of Wonder Woman once again, she is transported back to World War II. Disguised as the relatively unknown Super Hero Miss America, she shares an adventure with Hippolyta in the hopes of not damaging the time stream.

QUEEN NO MORE

While serving the JSA and fulfilling her role of Wonder Woman, Hippolyta slowly finds herself drawing further and further away from her responsibilities to the Amazon people—and her subjects notice. Given a choice between returning to rule or abdicating her throne and remaining in the role of Wonder Woman, Hippolyta casts aside her crown and rejoins the Justice Society.

Wonder Woman (Vol. 2) #185 (Nov. 2002) During a time travel trip, Princess Diana is disguised as Miss America.

> "Hear me Amazons! *I forsake my crown and my throne!*"
>
> HIPPOLYTA

Wonder Woman (Vol. 2) #172 (Sep. 2001)
Diana holds her dying mother, begging her to be strong.

WORTHY OF HER TITLE

During an invasion of Earth by the alien Imperiex and his army, Diana is injured in battle. Though she lacks the level of her daughter's god-granted powers, Hippolyta will not flee the battle. And when she witnesses her daughter in danger, the former queen flings herself onto the back of an Imperiex Probe, which explodes and kills Hippolyta in brutal fashion.

Resurrected Royal

Hippolyta is later reborn at the hands of Circe, who takes the opportunity to fuse a part of her own essence into Hippolyta's soul, making the queen bloodthirsty and warlike. Her time as Wonder Woman has passed, but her heroic sacrifices are never forgotten.

Amazons Attack (Vol. 1) #1 (Jun. 2007)
Diana expresses surprise at the sight of Hippolyta.

Wonder Woman (Vol. 2) #131 (Mar. 1998)
Hippolyta quickly finds happiness as Wonder Woman of the 1940s.

ARTEMIS

An Amazon from the Egyptian tribe of Bana-Mighdall, Artemis is known for her intensity and fierce nature. She first met Diana as a rival— even briefly replacing her as the new Wonder Woman. Over time she has become a noble ally to the Princess.

A skilled warrior, Artemis has trained to use her long hair as a weapon.

Artemis' jewelry and clothes reflect her heritage as a member of the Bana-Mighdall.

DATA FILE

FIRST APPEARANCE: *Wonder Woman* (Vol. 2) #90 (Sep. 1994)

OCCUPATION: Warrior, hero, leader

AFFILIATIONS: Amazons of Bana-Mighdall, Themyscira, Hellenders

POWERS/ABILITIES: Enhanced strength, speed, endurance

ALTERNATES: In a previous reality, Artemis was known as Orana. She died in her role as a replacement Wonder Woman.

SECOND CHANCE

Though Artemis was briefly chosen to become the new Wonder Woman, her time in that role did not last long. Thought to have been killed in battle, Artemis' spirit lived on in the underworld where she became a demon hunter. This role eventually led the fallen Amazon to Diana's side once more, where she assumed the mantle of mentor and teacher to the second Wonder Girl.

"I have trained my whole life to resist any amount of pain!"

ARTEMIS OF BANA-MIGHDALL

ORIGIN

The Amazons of Bana-Mighdall were originally led by Antiope, sister of Hippolyta. After the Amazons narrowly escaped conquer at the hand of Hercules, Antiope and her followers abandoned the Gods of Olympus and traveled to Egypt. Centuries later, Artemis was born as a member of this tribe.

In occupied Greece, Helena Kosmatos' mother suffered a heart attack and died when she found out that her son, Michael, was collaborating with the Nazis. The teenage Helena became enraged, swearing vengeance upon her brother. Her anger attracted the attention of the Furies of legend—deities whose role was to see vengeance served. The Fury Tisiphone granted Helena a fraction of her own power, and the hero Fury was born.

> *"Mother? I did this for you."*
> FURY

BEST INTENTIONS

Serving with the Young All-Stars, Fury was a troubled teenager—having difficulty controlling the Spirit of Vengeance that now dwelled within her. Despite this, Fury became a true hero and helped the All-Star Squadron defeat numerous enemies. Eventually, Fury encountered Hippolyta, Queen of the Amazons, and became infatuated with her as a mother figure.

DATA FILE

REAL NAME: Helena Kosmatos

FIRST APPEARANCE: *Infinity, Inc.* (Vol. 1) #35 (Feb. 1987)

OCCUPATION: Hero, Spirit of Vengeance

AFFILIATIONS: All-Star Squadron, Young All-Stars, Justice Society of America

POWERS/ABILITIES: Superhuman strength, speed, heat vision, immortality

ALTERNATES: Helena's daughter was Lyta Hall, who in the pre-Crisis universe was the daughter of Earth-Two's Wonder Woman.

Fury's hair has slowly turned from blonde to white since she acquired her powers.

Fury's yellow-gold armor is magical and aids her powers.

FURY

Given great power by the Furies of Greek legend, young Helena Kosmatos was transformed from an orphaned teenager into a superpowered warrior. She soon became a member of the 1940's junior team called the Young All-Stars.

BY JOHN BYRNE

WONDER WOMAN
(VOLUME 2)
#135

THE TWISTED FATE OF WONDER WOMAN'S SECRET SISTER!

As the ripples of the DC Universe relaunch continue to be felt, the original Wonder Girl's origins are altered and revamped. Donna Troy's identity has been renewed so many times that even she has lost track of who she is. This story aims to set things straight.

JULY 1998

MAIN CHARACTERS:
Wonder Woman • Donna Troy • Hippolyta

SUPPORTING CHARACTERS:
Magala • Philippus • Artemis • Cassie Sandsmark • The Flash • Merlin • Mike Schorr • Jason Blood

MAIN LOCATIONS:
Themyscira • Hell • Mount Olympus

1 While Princess Diana has been granted the station of Goddess of Truth and is bound to a pledge of non-intervention with the mortal world, her mother Hippolyta is serving as Wonder Woman. The Queen of the Amazons has just discovered that the original Wonder Girl, Donna Troy, is being held in eternal torment by a creature named Dark Angel.

2 The truth of Donna's origins is revealed. She is a doppelgänger of Wonder Woman, created using a magical mirror when Diana was a teenager. Dark Angel kidnapped Donna to torture Hippolyta, not realizing that the target of her wrath was not the actual princess. With two versions of the Flash at her side, Hippolyta journeys into Hell to save her pseudo-daughter.

3 Meanwhile, Cassie Sandsmark, in her guise as Wonder Girl, is also traveling into Hell, along with the Amazon Artemis and Merlin the wizard, among others. Their mission is to save Cassie's mother, Helena, and occult expert Jason Blood from the vile clutches of the legendary witch Morgan le Fey.

4 Unable to physically intervene, Princess Diana watches helplessly from Olympus. Desperate to aid Donna Troy, she sends along the only thing she can to her sister —a sense of inspiration. Recalling her time as Super Hero, Donna summons the powers she once held and her courage long buried, and leaps her way across the inferno.

5 Artemis strikes down Morgan, thus freeing Jason Blood from the curse of Etrigan. Meanwhile, Dark Angel mocks Queen Hippolyta for being so helpless against her magic—for it is only a similarly mystical force that can hurt Dark Angel in Hell.

6 Donna Troy, free from her prison, intervenes between Hippolyta and Dark Angel, grasping the mystical villain with a touch that turns the evil magic back upon the sorceress. Although Donna's touch is killing Dark Angel, the wrathful entity swears final vengeance, destroying Donna's mind as a last hateful act.

"It was at least a dozen lifetimes ago, but I fought alongside **Robin**, and **Kid Flash**, and **Aqualad**... And I remember the things I could do!"

DONNA TROY

THE JUSTICE LEAGUE INTERNATIONAL

After the events of the great Crisis, the history of the Justice League of America is cosmically rewritten. Wonder Woman, having arrived from Themyscira years after the League formed, is no longer a founding member. The original team has already disbanded, and now a new team—one with a more international approach to heroics—has arisen: the JLI.

ROCKET RED

Dmitri Pushkin is a good-natured Russian hero who fights for justice while wearing an advanced battle suit. He moved to the JLE from the JLI, hoping to be closer to his family.

GUY GARDNER

One of Earth's Green Lanterns, Guy Gardner is well known for his aggressive attitude and extremist views. Consequently, almost everyone who works with Guy ends up hating him.

EXPANDING HEROICS

Shortly after its inception, the JLI split into two groups—the Justice League of America and the Justice League of Europe. The post-Crisis Wonder Woman is briefly a member of the JLE.

CAPTAIN ATOM

The quantum-powered Captain Atom was projected through time from the 1960s, when he absorbed the energy of a nuclear explosion. He leads the Justice League of Europe.

MAX LORD

A brilliant businessman with a secret power to control minds, Maxwell Lord manipulates governments and heroes alike. Max is financier of this version of the Justice League International.

BOOSTER GOLD

A member of the JLI's American branch, Booster Gold was a janitor in the 25th century. He stole a power suit and time travel equipment in order to travel back to the present and become a hero.

POWER GIRL

Power Girl had thought she was a Kryptonian cousin of Superman from a parallel reality, but after the Crisis, she no longer knew who she really was—as no parallel realities were said to exist. Instead, she is believed to be a descendent of a great Atlantean sorcerer.

ELONGATED MAN

A would-be detective who owes his stretching powers to a super-concentrated essence of a rare fruit. Ralph Dibny joined the JLE in part because of his and his jet-setting wife Sue's love of travel.

THE FLASH

Wally West, a former sidekick to Barry Allen, has become the Flash. Wally hopes his time in the JLE will give him the positive experience his mentor had in the JLA.

METAMORPHO

Paid to retrieve the Orb of Ra from a pyramid, Rex Mason was knocked unconscious and left for dead near a radioactive meteorite. The exposure altered his body and he soon became a shape-shifting hero.

BLUE BEETLE

Inventor and millionaire Ted Kord became the Blue Beetle after his mentor—the original hero to use that name—was killed. A skilled fighter with an arsenal of weapons, the second Blue Beetle has no superpowers.

ANIMAL MAN

Buddy Baker can take on the abilities of any animal. He did not stay long with the JLE, as family issues prevented him from staying in Europe.

TERRIFYING TORMENTORS

Not content with gaining money or power, many of Wonder Woman's foes also seek to inflict pain. The Dark Age of comics—when the DC Universe undergoes its most brutal evolution—is a time where these foes come to prominence.

> *"Once upon a time, I banished you... so that I would be the fairest in the land. Apparently, I must do so again."*
> QUEEN OF FABLES

QUEEN OF FABLES

The Queen of Fables was a sorceress from another dimension who found herself exiled to Earth. As the embodiment of an evil fairytale, she drew power from fictional worlds within books. After being awoken from her centuries-long slumber, the Queen set her sights on Wonder Woman and the Justice League of America, mistaking the Amazon for Snow White. Wonder Woman defeated the Queen by lassoing her. She was imprisoned once more within a book—the US Tax Code.

THE WHITE MAGICIAN

Claiming to be hundreds of years old, the White Magician believed himself to have once been a hero. By the time he encountered Wonder Woman, he had been driven mad, and his racist and elitist world views repulsed the Amazon. With his powers waning, the White Magician sold his soul for increased magical strength. He used this dark gift to steal the life force of others, transforming himself into a demonic entity. Wonder Woman eventually defeated the White Magician, who, after the battle, was consumed by his own hellfire and turned to ash.

DECAY

The statue that became Decay started life in a similar fashion to Wonder Woman. Phobos—son of Ares—formed her from malevolent matter taken from the Gorgon Medusa's heart. Phobos sent Decay to the Kapatelis' house where Wonder Woman was staying. She attacked Vanessa Kapatelis and forcibly aged her. She then rampaged through Boston, spreading fear and terror in her wake. Wonder Woman destroyed her, reducing her to dust, but she later returned.

DARK ANGEL

Once a fearsome foe of Wonder Woman's mother Hippolyta, the Dark Angel turned her attention toward the young girl she believed to be Princess Diana, but instead captured Diana's magical doppelgänger, Donna Troy. Dark Angel used her evil powers to torture Donna by forcing her to live many lifetimes, with each one ending in tragedy. Donna's memories of her previous lives were erased and her history reinvented. In an attempt to rescue Donna, Hippolyta traveled into Hell, where she was being held by Dark Angel. Finally, the evil entity was defeated.

MAXWELL LORD

Max Lord first came to prominence when he created an alternate version of the Justice League: the Justice League International. Eventually Max's powers of psychic manipulation were discovered, as were his plans to kill all superhumans. When confronted, Max shot and killed former JLI member the Blue Beetle, and threatened to use Superman as an instrument of destruction. With no alternative, Wonder Woman snapped the villain's neck.

With the dawn of the 21st Century, the Amazon Princess' journey from peaceful messenger to militaristic, heroic warrior became more and more apparent. This was a Wonder Woman who understood that in the battle of good and evil, difficult choices must often be made.

THE MODERN AGE

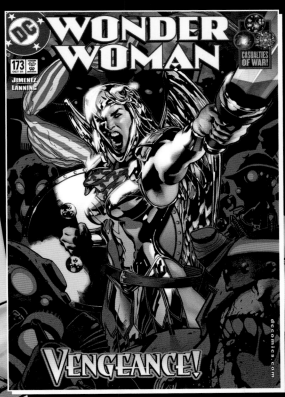

Wonder Woman (Vol. 2) #173 (Oct. 2001)
Wonder Woman joins forces with evil god
Darkseid, to destroy a greater threat.

Wonder Woman (Vol. 2) #213
(Apr. 2005) The Amazon warrior
uses Medusa's head to
defeat Zeus' guard.

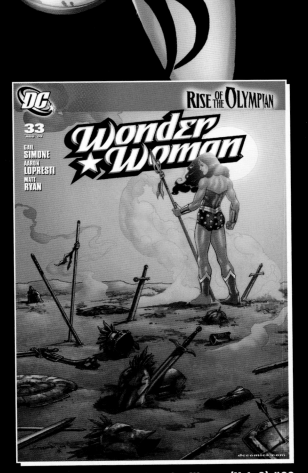

Wonder Woman (Vol. 3) #33
(Aug. 2009) Wonder Woman kills an
Olympian god, and rejects Zeus.

As the clock ticks toward the Modern Age, the legacy of Wonder Woman is evident through both the heroes and villains she inspires. Hope, heroism, and feminism: all are a part of Wonder Woman's legacy. She is a hero who repeatedly casts aside her own happiness and safety to ensure others may find peace and love.

SOCIAL JUSTICE

Inspired by the heroic actions of Wonder Woman, youth groups devoted to raising money for charity and building community outreach programs spring up around the globe. They operate under a name that honors Wonder Woman's deceased friend and publicist, Myndi Mayer.

Wonder Woman (Vol. 2) #196 (Nov. 2003)

SISTERS IN SPIRIT

As Wonder Woman faces the dead body of her future self—reanimated and powered through corruption and murder—she finds her greatest allies to be those who are inspired directly by her heroism. The first and second Wonder Girls stand with Diana in full Amazon armor, the living legacies of Princess Diana, ready to defend their sister to the last.

Wonder Woman (Vol. 3) #28 (Mar. 2009)

THE RETURN OF A FRIEND

Despite being manipulated and tortured by several super-villains over the years, one of Wonder Woman's closest friends, Vanessa Kapatelis, graduates from Valedictorian College. It is the inspiration of Wonder Woman that has driven the young girl to reformation and physical rehabilitation. Even though she has never become a Wonder Girl, Vanessa has grown to fully embody the Amazon ideal of personal growth and courage.

Wonder Woman (Vol. 3) #600 (Aug. 2010)

INSPIRED ALLIES

After Wonder Woman is forced to execute a master criminal to save Superman, she makes the difficult choice of walking away from her identity for a year. In that time, Donna Troy—the original Wonder Girl—keeps alive the name and appearance of Wonder Woman, honoring her mentor's message and memory. When the original Amazon hero returns and stands alone against an army of villains, a horde of Diana's superpowered friends arrive to save the day. This is the legacy the Princess of Themyscira has inspired. From sidekicks to Super Heroes, they stand together with Wonder Woman. Each is inspired by—and willing to help spread—the Amazon Princess's message of peace and liberty for all humanity.

Wonder Woman (Vol. 3) #600 (Aug. 2010)

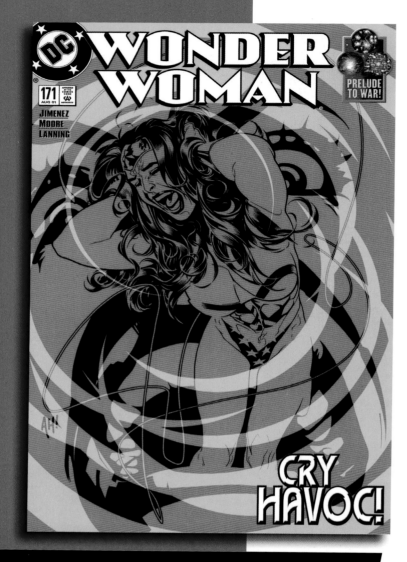

WONDER WOMAN
(VOLUME 2)
#171

THE SONIC SWANSONG OF A WOULD-BE WONDER GIRL AND FORMER FRIEND.

AUGUST 2001

As Wonder Woman makes the subtle shift from the Dark Age of comics into the Modern Age, her own past comes back to haunt her. Vanessa Kapatelis—a character who had mostly been absent of late—comes back to avenge her perceived abandonment.

MAIN CHARACTERS:
Wonder Woman

SUPPORTING CHARACTERS:
Cheetah • Cassie Sandsmark • Helena Sandsmark • Hippolyta • Sebastian Ballesteros • Vanessa Kapatelis • Circe

MAIN LOCATIONS:
Gateway City • New York

1 While meeting in New York, Diana and Hippolyta discuss the recent events that have led to both of them no longer holding their positions as Amazonian royalty. Their conversation quickly dissolves into an argument over the former Amazon Queen failing to properly address the needs of her people.

2 At the same time, a winged figure streaks across the sky toward the Sandsmark residence. It strikes a sonic blast at the heart of the building, destroying the home, which was fortunately empty at the time. Elsewhere, the winged figure's progress is being monitored by a man called Sebastian Ballesteros.

3 The winged figure moves on to another target. Meanwhile, Ballesteros orders his lab technicians to continue psychically uploading information to keep the winged figure hostile and aggressive. The silver-clad being moves on to attack the museum where Helena Sandsmark works.

4 The attacker flies off to another location—this time the school of Cassie Sandsmark, who is also Wonder Girl. With a violent sonic scream, the building is ripped in two, killing one of Cassie's friends. Enraged, Wonder Girl sees the person behind the attacks. It is Wonder Woman's former friend Vanessa Kapatelis, now transformed into the cybernetically enhanced super-villain known as the Silver Swan.

5 Vanessa defeats Wonder Girl, but before she can move in for the kill, Wonder Woman arrives on the scene to defend her young protégée. Diana is horrified to see the identity of the attacker, instinctively knowing that someone is manipulating Vanessa. Before she can get through to the girl, she is attacked by Sebastian Ballesteros, now revealed to be a male incarnation of Cheetah.

6 The villains escape Wonder Woman's wrath through the power of the sorceress Circe, the brains behind the attack. With a mocking smile, Circe bids Diana farewell, knowing that Vanessa's conversion will haunt Wonder Woman. Before Wonder Woman can even begin to process what has occurred, Darkseid—the ruler of Apokolips—attacks Earth, and all other matters must be put aside.

"I should have been Wonder Girl!"

VANESSA KAPATELIS

THEMYSCIRAN EMBASSY

The Embassy of Themyscira is located in New York City on the East Coast of the United States of America. It serves as an occasional place of residence and a base of operations for Wonder Woman. With its team of support staff, the Themysciran Embassy allows the Amazon to continue her mission to bring peace to the world.

EXPOSING SECRETS

The embassy houses several full-time staff members, each carefully chosen to help the Princess represent the global needs of the Amazons. This has become increasingly important following the exposure of the once-hidden island of Themyscira off the East Coast of America.

RACHEL KEAST

Head of the embassy's legal team, Rachel Keast specializes in international law. She takes her job very seriously, and her forthright attitude and fearless convictions make her well suited to untying the impossible legal knots that Wonder Woman's activities frequently create.

JONAH MCCARTHY

Hired to represent the embassy's legal needs, Jonah McCarthy was a secret agent for the government spy agency known as Checkmate. Identified by the Amazon and released from service, Jonah returned to his position in Checkmate. He was later shot and killed during a raid on an installation belonging to terror group Kobra.

PETER GARIBALDI

Peter Garibaldi is the press secretary for the Themysciran Embassy, and thus oversees media affairs. He resides on the premises with his two young sons, Bobby and Martin.

ALANA DOMINGUEZ

Alana Dominguez serves as Wonder Woman's secretary. She is tasked with managing the general staff of the organization and juggling Wonder Woman's ever-changing and hectic schedule.

FERDINAND

Often identified as a Minotaur, Ferdinand is not from Minos, but from Kythos. Consequently, he is (as he constantly reminds people) a Kythotaur. Ferdinand serves as the embassy's chef, cooking exclusively vegetarian dishes for Wonder Woman and the staff.

141

EYES OF THE GORGON

The world has changed, and the Gods have found that their old roles no longer apply. Thus Athena plans to claim the throne of Olympus from her increasingly irrational father, Zeus—a dangerous gambit that could unleash destruction onto all.

> " *I will **not** be cheated! **Not** again! **Look at me!**"*
>
> MEDUSA

REBIRTH

In a bid to attack Athena, Poseidon instructs Circe the sorceress and Gorgon sisters Stheno and Euryale to resurrect the long-dead body of his former lover, the snake-haired Medusa. It is a slow process, but eventually the most famous Gorgon returns. Medusa seeks revenge against Athena, who had cursed her—a revenge she will take out upon Athena's chosen champion: Diana.

Wonder Woman (Vol. 2) #205 (Aug. 2004) *Circe uses ancient witchcraft to resurrect the Gorgon, Medusa.*

Wonder Woman (Vol. 2) #210 (Jan. 2005) *Wonder Woman blinds herself with snake venom.*

A TERRIBLE PRICE

Medusa wastes little time attacking Wonder Woman and her allies at the Themysciran Embassy. Targeting the young son of staff member Peter Garibaldi, she turns him to stone. Athena later tells Diana that this was a necessary price to pay.

Wonder Woman (Vol. 2) #209 (Dec. 2004) *Snake-haired Medusa unleashes her wrath.*

BLIND DEDICATION

Enraged at the young life lost under her own watch, heartbroken that the cost of her friendship must always come at a high price, Wonder Woman dons her battle armor and faces the Gorgon on live television. While being recorded, the Amazon proves the depth of her dedication and uses the venom from one of Medusa's snakes to destroy her own eyes—ensuring the Gorgon cannot turn her to stone.

Wonder Woman (Vol. 2) #212 (Mar. 2005) *For the blind Wonder Woman, it is a bittersweet victory.*

HOLLOW VICTORY

Despite being blinded during their battle, Wonder Woman beheads her enemy, thereby ending Medusa's threat forever. However, the victory is bittersweet. For though millions of television viewers have been spared the face of the Gorgon, a young child still died for the cause. That price is not one the Amazon can easily forget.

Wonder Woman (Vol. 2) #217 (July 2005) *Peter's son, and Wonder Woman's sight, are restored.*

A HAPPY ENDING

Athena eventually claims the throne of Zeus. Her first act is to send her champion Wonder Woman to recover Hermes from the realm of the dead and claim Hades' domain for Ares. When the Amazon is successful, Athena restores Peter Garibaldi's son, and Wonder Woman's vision.

Wonder Woman (Vol. 2) #210 (Jan. 2005) *Stabbed in the side, Wonder Woman fights on.*

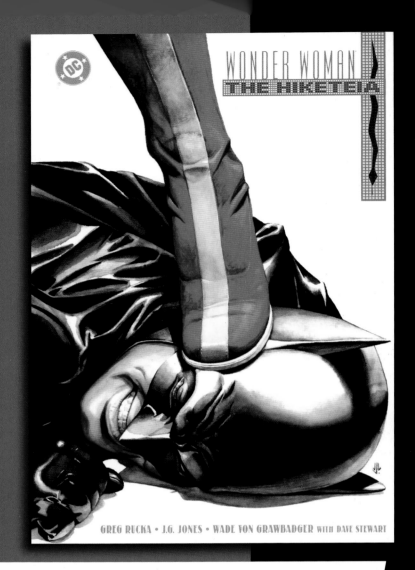

GREG RUCKA • J.G. JONES • WADE VON GRAWBADGER with DAVE STEWART

AUGUST 2002

MAIN CHARACTERS:
Wonder Woman • Batman •
Danielle Wellys

SUPPORTING CHARACTERS:
The Erinyes—the three minor
Gods of Vengeance

MAIN LOCATIONS:
Themysciran Embassy

WONDER WOMAN THE HIKETEIA

WHEN HONOR AND DUTY CLASH WITH JUSTICE THERE CAN BE NO WINNERS.

Wonder Woman is put to the test when her honor compels her to protect a murderer from Batman's justice. The story reminds the reader of Wonder Woman's original role as an outsider and defender of women, rather than as a Super Hero who defends the law.

1 Pursued by Batman through Gotham City, a young female murderer named Danielle Wellys manages to escape the Dark Knight's justice by plunging into Gotham Bay. In time, she makes her way to New York City, to the entrance of the Themysciran Embassy, home of Wonder Woman.

2 Danielle performs a ritual of supplication to gain Wonder Woman's protection. The Amazon accepts the young fugitive into her own life without question, as is the way with the ancient Greek custom of Hiketeia. To an Amazon, the ritual is as law: binding and inflexible.

3 Unseen by all save Wonder Woman, the Erinyes watch over the proceedings, constantly lurking in the shadows and threatening retribution should Wonder Woman fail to honor the supplicant properly. Shortly after, Batman tracks Danielle to Wonder Woman's residence within the Embassy, demanding that she turn over the killer to him.

4 After Wonder Woman defends Danielle against Batman, the accused murderer tearfully confesses the nature of her crimes to her host. Danielle's sister was forced onto a destructive and deadly path by corrupt men who sidestepped the law to avoid blame. When the inevitable happened and her sister died, she took revenge according to ancient Greek laws.

5 Overwhelmed with misery and guilt, Danielle flees into the night. Batman soon finds the terrified girl and tries to apprehend her, an act that once again leads the Dark Knight and Wonder Woman to clash. Batman attempts to use the ritual of Hiketeia to prevent Wonder Woman from stopping him, but is refused for abusing the spirit of the custom.

*"I offer **myself** in supplication."*

BATMAN

6 Seeing that the end result of her actions will only lead to conflict, Danielle decides to take her own life. When both Batman and Wonder Woman attempt to stop her, the Erinyes intervene and the avenging killer throws herself to her own death.

THE EXECUTION OF MAX LORD

While investigating the death of former Justice League member, Blue Beetle, Wonder Woman and her allies uncover a conspiracy that threatens the superhuman community. Manipulated and beaten, the Amazon warrior must make a difficult choice.

*"I'm the **Black King**. I'm your **ruler**."*

MAXWELL LORD

SPY LORD

While uncovering the details of Blue Beetle's death, Wonder Woman and her friends are monitored by a former ally—Max Lord, entrepreneur and former manager of the Justice League. Lord has acquired spy technology built by Batman—a semi-sentient satellite called Brother Eye.

Adventures of Superman #642 (Sep. 2005) *Wonder Woman realizes the depths of the villain's plans.*

Wonder Woman (Vol. 2) #219 (Sep. 2005) *Max Lord revels in his power.*

ONE MAN ARMY CORPS

Knowing that the investigation into the murder of the Blue Beetle will lead the Justice League to his organization, Max Lord initiates the next stage of his anti-metahuman campaign. He launches an army of killing machines—OMACs—each programmed to destroy the superhuman beings that Maxwell Lord is convinced will one day rise up against humanity.

The OMAC Project #5 (Oct. 2005) *The OMACs are activated.*

MAXIMUM CONTROL

Max Lord uses mind control to drive Superman to the brink of insanity. Under this spell, Superman hospitalizes Batman and battles Wonder Woman to a standstill. Using her Golden Lasso to divine the truth, the Amazon learns that the only way to end Superman's murderous rampage is the death of his controller. With no options left, the Amazon champion breaks Lord's neck.

The OMAC Project #4 (Sep. 2005)
Wonder Woman is compelled to kill Lord if she is to save others.

The OMAC Project #5 (Oct. 2005)
Rocket Red sacrifices himself to save his fellow heroes.

HEROES FALL

Even without Maxwell Lord's guidance, his army of mercenary drones carries out his murderous wishes, hunting down and killing Super Heroes. It is up to Wonder Woman and her friends to use the technology of the Blue Beetle to stop the threat.

PUBLIC EYE

The execution of Max Lord is not an easy decision for Wonder Woman to make. It costs her the trust of her closest friends, and after the death is publicized by the sinister Brother Eye, she also loses the trust of the public she has sworn to protect.

The OMAC Project #6 (Nov. 2005) Brother Eye broadcasts Max's execution.

147

As humanity rebuilds after a brutal war,
Wonder Woman questions her place
with the Amazons.

Wonder Woman (Vol. 3) #13 (Dec. 2007)

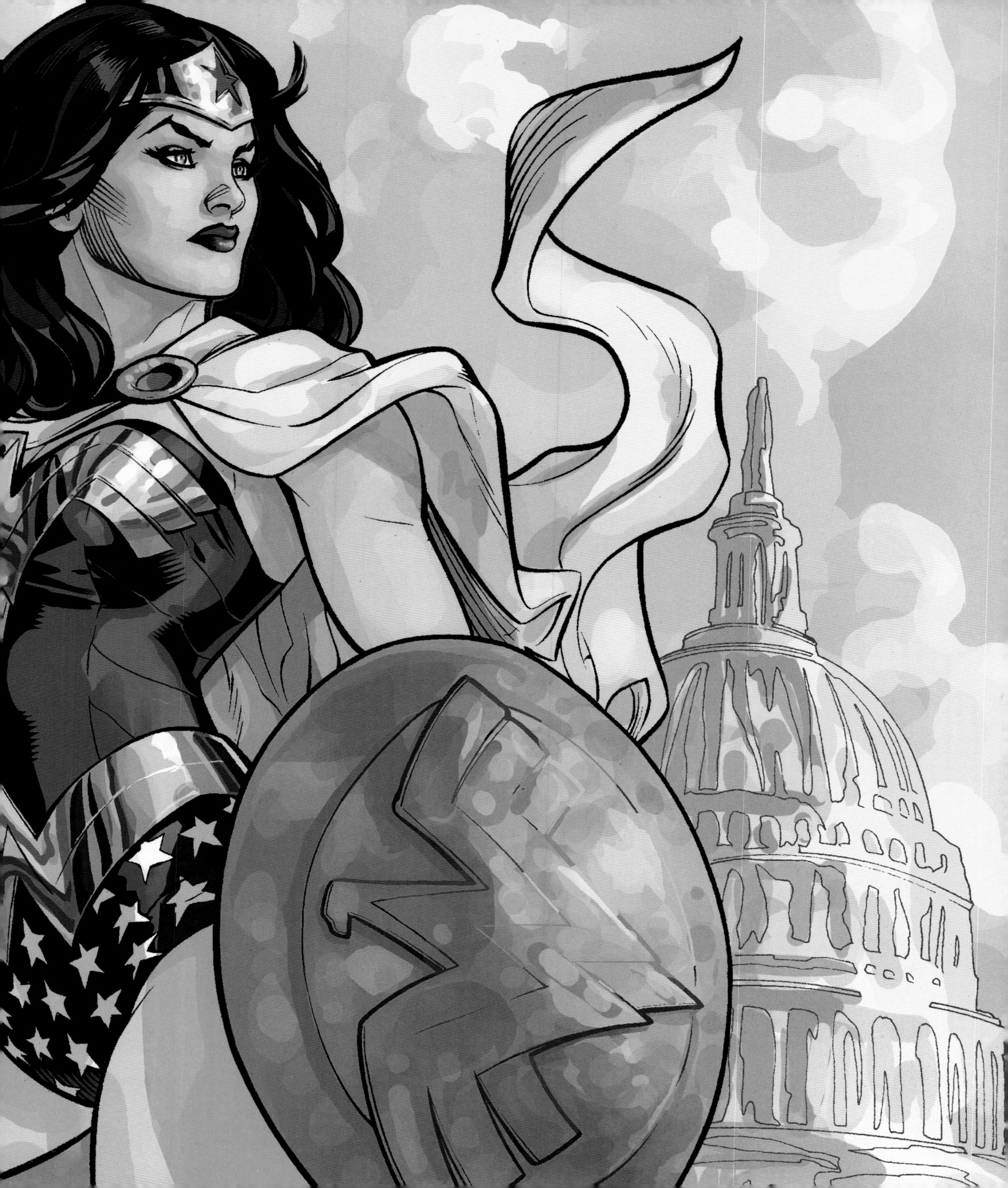

DIANA PRINCE—SECRET AGENT

After the execution of Maxwell Lord, Wonder Woman disappears from the public eye for a year. Unwilling to give up her role as a Super Hero, the Amazon creates a new identity for this era. It is one that has not been used since before the Crisis event—in another reality by a different incarnation of Wonder Woman—Diana Prince.

Wonder Woman (Vol. 3) #2 (Sep. 2006) Wonder Woman, in the guise of Diana Prince, clashes with government agent Nemesis—Tom Tresser—on their first meeting.

EMPLOYED

Working with the Department of Metahuman Affairs and partnered with the secret agent known as Nemesis, Diana Prince embarks on missions that help protect the globe from superhuman threats.

Wonder Woman (Vol. 3) #2 (Sep. 2006) Donna Troy takes over from Diana as Wonder Woman.

SISTER ACT

In her sister's absence, Donna Troy takes on the mantle of Wonder Woman and struggles to keep the forces of evil at bay. Sensing something has changed, the villains gather together and attempt to flush out the real Wonder Woman, capturing Donna in the process.

UNLIKELY HERO

With things looking dire, Diana decides she must return to her Super Hero identity. But before she can transform back into Wonder Woman, a new arrival interrupts her—Hercules. Taking on the role of a Super Hero, Hercules dispatches the super-villains, gaining Diana's trust in the process. But it's all just a ruse to disguise his true allegiances.

Wonder Woman (Vol. 3) #2 (Sep. 2006) Hercules arrives and announces that he will take care of the villains.

> "Your reign as Gods on Earth **is over**."
> WONDER WOMAN

Wonder Woman (Vol. 3) Annual #1 (Nov. 2007) *Diana battles foes including Cheetah, Doctor Psycho, Queen Clea, and Angle Man.*

Wonder Woman (Vol. 3) #1 (Aug. 2006) *Wonder Woman joins the Department of Metahuman Affairs as Diana Prince.*

DOUBLE TROUBLE

Circe arrives and takes Diana's powers. It is revealed that the sorceress and Hercules are partners who plan to rule the world. Diana recovers her powers and becomes Wonder Woman once again, only to be ambushed by all her enemies at once. Luckily, she is joined by a liberated Donna, Cassie, and other Super Heroes.

MORTALLY WOUNDED

The enemies defeated, Wonder Woman discovers a lasting gift from Circe. A spell that causes her to lose her powers when in the guise of Diana Prince. Rather than run from this new vulnerability, Wonder Woman embraces it, deciding that it makes her closer to the mortals she has sworn to protect.

Wonder Woman (Vol. 3) Annual #1 (Nov. 2007) *Wonder Woman finds that she can be wounded when she is Diana Prince.*

COMRADES IN ARMS

During the Modern Age, Wonder Woman re-establishes herself as the emissary from Themyscira and manages the embassy of the Amazons. Since the Crisis event, she has forged new friendships, as well as nurturing old ones.

*"Why me, Diana? You're a **freaking princess and a goddess** and I... I'm so not."*

Tom Tresser

ACHILLES WARKILLER

Initially at odds with Wonder Woman, Achilles was created by Zeus in a mystical bonfire, with the intention that the superpowered soldier would serve as a figure of hope for the warrior Olympians. Zeus wanted to replicate the success of Wonder Woman's creation, and in doing so ripped out the heart of the Hawaiian God Kane Milohai and infused it with his own mystical lightning. Despite this murderous beginning, Achilles is an honorable warrior, who respects Wonder Woman tremendously.

TOM TRESSER

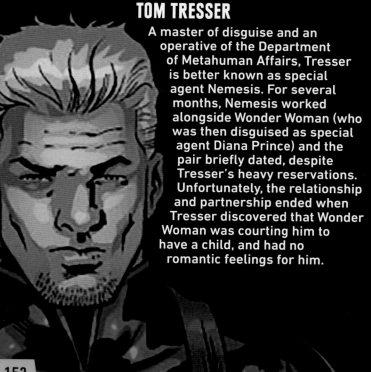

A master of disguise and an operative of the Department of Metahuman Affairs, Tresser is better known as special agent Nemesis. For several months, Nemesis worked alongside Wonder Woman (who was then disguised as special agent Diana Prince) and the pair briefly dated, despite Tresser's heavy reservations. Unfortunately, the relationship and partnership ended when Tresser discovered that Wonder Woman was courting him to have a child, and had no romantic feelings for him.

GORILLA KNIGHTS

Lead by Tolifhar—a gorilla formerly under command of the renegade Gorilla Grodd—these knights were genetically modified white-furred gorillas conditioned to fight superhumans. Originally from the hidden Gorilla City, they were sent to fight Wonder Woman, but befriended her after she persuaded them to defect. They lived with Wonder Woman in her apartment in Washington, D.C. and served loyally at her side when the need arose. Eventually, the gorillas' honorable actions in service to the Amazons led Solovar, King of Gorilla City, to invite the Gorilla Knights to return home.

SARGE STEEL

Sarge Steel spent some time serving as the liaison between the American president and the metahuman community. He eventually transferred into a role as the head of the Department of Metahuman Affairs. Following the death of Maxwell Lord at the hands of Wonder Woman, Steel became distrustful of the Amazon hero. This was despite the fact that he was unwittingly employing her under her identity as Diana Prince. After being attacked by both Circe and Doctor Psycho, Sarge Steel was succeeded in his role at the DMA by Steve Trevor.

TREVOR BARNES

Trevor Barnes was a human rights advocate and field director for the United Nations Rural Development Organization. Wonder Woman and Barnes dated and shared many adventures together. Unfortunately, their relationship ended tragically when Barnes, who had been selected by the Earth mother Gaea to save the world, used his own body to imprison the evil entity known as the Shattered God. This act saved the world, but caused Trevor Barnes to age rapidly and die soon after.

TITANIC TEAMWORK!

In the post-Crisis Universe, a brand-new incarnation of the Justice League rises up, with seven Super Heroes of the merged reality coming together to defend the Earth from alien invasions and destructive evil forces.

*"Leave this world **alone!**"*

WONDER WOMAN

DEADLY DUEL

After learning of a prophecy that foretells the death of her teammates, Wonder Woman betrays the members of the Justice League and faces the threat of an ancient dragon, Drakul Karfang, alone. Despite being mortally wounded in the process, she manages to defeat the evil monster. Her teammates are able to rally in time to save the fallen Amazon from the cost of her heroic sacrifice.

JLA: A League of One **(Nov. 2000)** *Wonder Woman single-handedly faces the might of Drakul Karfang—and wins.*

JLA (Vol. 1) #54 (Jul. 2001) *Her body reduced to the clay from which it was created, Wonder Woman's true form is revealed as the Spirit of Truth.*

ALTER EGO

Wonder Woman's allies in the JLA are split from their alternate secret identities by alien attackers from the sixth dimension, known as the Cathexis. The Amazon chooses to trick the enemy into using a weapon—an energy called ID—on her, challenging the Cathexis to divide a hero with no secret identity. The process frees Wonder Woman's spirit from her body, allowing her to save her friends.

JLA (Vol. 1) #75 (Jan. 2003) *Wonder Woman, Superman, and the Martian Manhunter pull the world free from danger.*

SAVING EARTH

With her Golden Lasso of Truth enchanted by the shaman Manitou Raven, Wonder Woman, helped by Superman and the Martian Manhunter, pulls the Earth free of a corrupted orbit. It is the culmination of a daring plan to stop Gamemnae—an evil sorceress from the distant past—who is determined to rise Atlantis from the depths of the sea, and turn its citizens into a conquering army.

JLA (Vol. 1) #4 (Apr. 1997) *High above Earth, Wonder Woman fights one-on-one with the red-eyed, white-skinned Martian named Primaid.*

MARTIAN INFILTRATION

Disguising themselves as heroes, several White Martians attempt to surreptitiously conquer the Earth under the guise of a team called the Hyperclan. Using their combined abilities, the Hyperclan nearly succeeds in brainwashing humanity. During the epic climax, Wonder Woman battles the White Martian known as Primaid in the upper atmosphere.

RISING TO THE OCCASION

While the JLA battles the destructive force of the Old Gods that is known as Mageddon, Wonder Woman leads an army of civilians—all of whom have been temporarily given vast powers—into battle. It is a desperate, last-ditch effort to save humanity from absolute destruction—one that will cost thousands of lives but is a small price to pay to save millions.

JLA (Vol. 1) #41 (May 2000) *Powered by a mutagenic field, the entire population of Earth gains Superman-like powers.*

WEAPONS OF WAR

As Wonder Woman herself is an icon of peace, it should come as no surprise that she would attract villains who stand as the living embodiments of war—both in the mortal plane and in the realm of the gods.

*"So **come forward**, guardians of humanity! Unleash your savage nature and stop us **if you dare!"***

ERIS

CYBORGIRL

LeTonya Charles had ruined her body through excessive use of dangerous, strength-enhancing narcotics. Her aunt, a brilliant scientist who had aided in the reconstruction of the hero Cyborg, managed to save LeTonya with powerful implants. LeTonya soon used her new body and the powers it granted as a weapon to commit crime. This path ultimately led her into direct conflict with Wonder Woman.

DEVASTATION

Molded from clay by the Titan Cronus, Devastation was created to be a mirror image of Wonder Woman. The freshly born villain soon discovered that Wonder Woman was her equal match, and chose instead to focus her energies on Cassie Sandsmark. Devastation manipulated the second Wonder Girl to battle her mentor, and later formed a team of young villains to fight Wonder Girl and her allies.

THE CHILDREN OF ARES

Ares has many children, some of whom have caused chaos on Earth. Deimos, the Greek God of Terror, is always ready to unleash evil upon humanity. He takes pride in aiding his father's plans to conquer the mortal realm. Phobos, the Greek God of Fear and Horror, has crossed Wonder Woman several times, notably when he possessed Batman and became the avatar of Fear. Eris, the Greek Goddess of Strife and Chaos, once used the Apple of Discord to sow distrust, turning the world against the Amazons.

GENOCIDE

At some point in the distant future, Ares, the God of War, acquires the dead body of Wonder Woman. With the assistance of the Secret Society of Super-Villains, he then collects soil samples from various locations on Earth where horrific acts of genocide have occurred. Through a combination of dark sorcery and mad science, a creature is brought to life. It is a sadistic monster known as Genocide, dedicated to the destruction of all—especially Wonder Woman.

SILVER SWAN

There have been three villains known as the Silver Swan, each one a product of the cruel manipulation of others. The most notable is Vanessa Kapatelis, who had spent her later teen years as one of Wonder Woman's closest friends. When Wonder Woman moved away, villains including Doctor Psycho and Circe began twisting and tormenting Vanessa's mind, and the young woman snapped. She was kidnapped, experimented on, and transformed into a mechanical monster, set on destroying her former hero.

FLASHPOINT—A NEW CRISIS

When The Flash (Barry Allen) runs back in time to stop his mother's murder, he creates a paradox that ripples across the Multiverse. Consequently, reality is altered. Allies become enemies and friends are forgotten—as Diana of Themyscira and Arthur of Atlantis discover as they plan to wed.

*"This isn't a parallel Earth or a mirror world... **this is home. This is real.**"*

THE FLASH

Wonder Woman and the Furies (Vol. 1) #1 (Aug. 2011) *During the ceremony, Hippolyta is killed by a trident thrown from the shadows.*

DEATH OF A MONARCH

Unfortunately, there are many among both Amazons and Atlanteans who oppose the union. An assassination is staged, which leads to the death of Queen Hippolyta. War between the Amazon and the Atlantean nations is now inevitable.

Flashpoint (Vol. 2) #2 (Aug. 2011) *Facing questions from Batman, Barry Allen realizes that the battles between the Amazons and the Atlanteans have really happened.*

Wonder Woman and the Furies (Vol. 1) #1 (Aug. 2011) *Diana and Arthur prepare to marry—and so unify their cultures.*

ROYAL WEDDING

In the Flashpoint reality, Diana is engaged to Arthur (Aquaman). Having met on the open sea when they were young, the pair decide that a wedding would bring unity to their similar peoples.

Wonder Woman and the Furies #2 (Sep. 2011) Diana puts on the helmet of the dead Atlantean queen, Mera.

Wonder Woman and the Furies #3 (Oct. 2011) Fighting for their own nations, Aquaman and Wonder Woman face each other in battle.

NO PRISONERS

The anger between the Amazons and Atlanteans leads to a brutal conflict and a great deal of blood is spilled. In the pursuit of victory for her people, Wonder Woman murders Mera—Aquaman's true love. In an act of unforgivable spite, Wonder Woman claims the helmet of her fallen foe.

CASUALTIES OF WAR

Deep into the war now, Atlanteans generate tidal waves and Amazons trigger earthquakes—leading to the deaths of millions of innocent civilians and the sinking of entire continents. The battle between Aquaman and Wonder Woman tears the world apart in the process. There are no survivors.

Flashpoint (Vol. 2) #5 (Oct. 2011) As Barry Allen tries to enter the timestream, a mysterious woman asks him to help unify the three separate timelines: DCU, Vertigo, and Wildstorm.

A NEW START

As the world comes to an end, Barry Allen gains the strength he needs to return back through time and stop his prior self from saving his mother's life. In doing so, he merges three divergent realities into a new whole—one that is familiar, yet different. It is a core of 52 closely layered realities, surrounded by an infinitely expanding Multiverse.

In the wake of the Flashpoint event, reality was altered, and it was time for a new incarnation of Wonder Woman. No longer a being shaped from clay, this Diana was the daughter of Zeus and Hippolyta. At the start of this era, Wonder Woman was unaware of her true origins. This led her story to become less focused on the message of peace and more oriented toward self-discovery.

THE NEW AGE

Wonder Woman (Vol. 4) #1 (Nov. 2011)
A new warrior for a new Olympian
war involving Zeus' offspring.

Wonder Woman (Vol. 4) #9 (July 2012)
Olympian guests arrive for
the wedding of Hades and Diana.

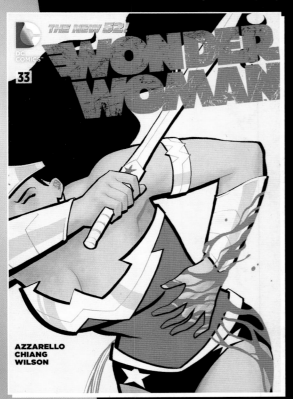

**Wonder Woman (Vol. 4) #33
(Sep. 2014)**
Stabbed by First Born, Wonder
Woman witnesses the destruction
of Paradise Island.

LINEAGE

In the wake of the Flashpoint event, Wonder Woman's journey shifts focus once more from heroism to self-discovery. With her Olympian lineage and a child of Zeus revealed, it is inevitable that Diana will fight to determine her own place among her family—the mighty Olympian Gods.

BODYGUARD OF THE GODS

When a young woman named Zola finds herself pregnant with Zeus' child, Wonder Woman must step into the role of bodyguard. Her role is to protect Zola from the vicious family of gods of which she is now a part. It is a race of those whose Olympian lineage grants them a birthright to the throne, and all the gods and demigods of Olympus are contestants.

Wonder Woman (Vol. 4) #1
(Nov. 2011)

AN UNLIKELY FATHER

Believing herself to be made of clay and given life, a lonely Princess Diana finds an unlikely father figure in Ares. The God of War takes her in and teaches her the way of combat. When the teenage Amazon is ordered to execute a fallen foe, rather than kill a helpless enemy, she stands against the guidance of her mentor, and risks alienating the only father figure she has ever known.

Wonder Woman (Vol. 4)
#0 (Nov. 2012)

ERRANT SON

Defying the will of his father, Orion of the New Gods abandons his mission to destroy the baby of Zola and Zeus. Instead, he joins Wonder Woman as an ally in her fight to save the infant child from the family of warring Olympian Gods.

Wonder Woman (Vol. 4) #22
(Sep. 2013)

WEIGHT OF RESPONSIBILITY

Wonder Woman has assumed the role of God of War from her father figure Ares and the mantle of Queen of Themyscira from her mother. However, she struggles with nightmares of what her new roles mean and how they will come to affect her future.

Wonder Woman (Vol. 4) #38 (Mar. 2015)

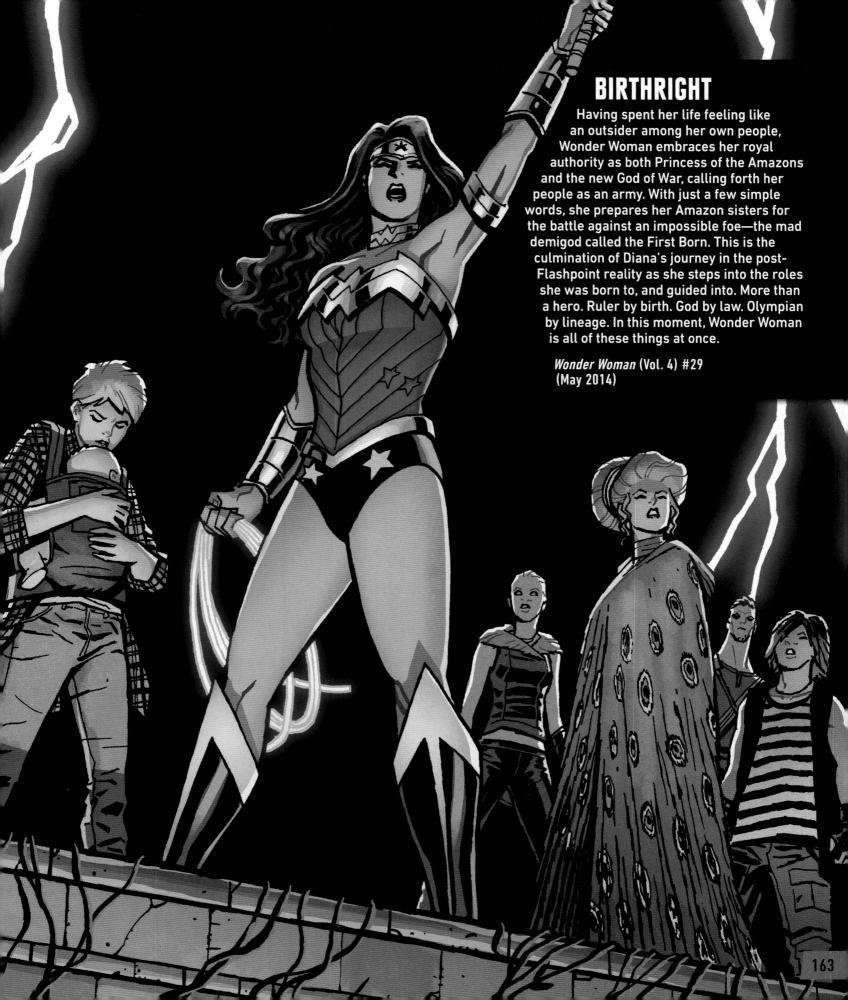

BIRTHRIGHT

Having spent her life feeling like an outsider among her own people, Wonder Woman embraces her royal authority as both Princess of the Amazons and the new God of War, calling forth her people as an army. With just a few simple words, she prepares her Amazon sisters for the battle against an impossible foe—the mad demigod called the First Born. This is the culmination of Diana's journey in the post-Flashpoint reality as she steps into the roles she was born to, and guided into. More than a hero. Ruler by birth. God by law. Olympian by lineage. In this moment, Wonder Woman is all of these things at once.

Wonder Woman (Vol. 4) #29
(May 2014)

NEW JUSTICE

When Darkseid invades the Earth, the greatest heroes of the universe band together to drive back the New God's assault. As well as a desperate battle to keep the Earth safe, the newly formed super-team must work together in harmony.

Justice League (Vol. 2) #3 (Jan. 2012) *Wonder Woman strikes at Darkseid's winged monsters.*

Alien Investigation

The struggle between the heroes escalates rapidly when Green Lantern calls the Flash for assistance. While four of the greatest heroes ever known battle each other in the streets, Wonder Woman leaves the care of the Federal Government—and the oversight of Steve Trevor—to investigate rumors of an attack on innocents by a winged creature in the capital.

Justice League (Vol. 2) #2 (Dec. 2011) *In Metropolis, an irate Superman easily breaks the chains made by Green Lantern, and goes on to attack Batman.*

MISTAKEN IDENTITY

After battling one of Darkseid's deadly parademons, Green Lantern and Batman seek extraterrestrial advice from another well-known alien—Superman. Having just battled another parademon, the Man of Steel is understandably confused by the appearance of the costumed heroes, and strikes against them under the misconception that they are the enemy.

EXTRATERRESTRIAL ATTACK

Superman and the others finally sort out their differences, only to be attacked by a horde of invading parademons. Hundreds of the strange demonic creatures emerge from various portals and fly at the Super Heroes. The attack extends across the world, potentially endangering all life on Earth. Luckily, Wonder Woman follows the creatures from Washington, D.C. and arrives among the other heroes just in time to turn the tide of the battle.

Justice League (Vol. 2) #3 (Jan. 2012) *Wonder Woman joins the Flash, Batman, Superman, Cyborg, Aquaman, and Green Lantern to fight the threat of Darkseid.*

> "This **world** belongs to **no one**. And **everyone**."
>
> WONDER WOMAN

Justice League (Vol. 2) #1 (Nov. 2011) The post-Flashpoint Justice League assembles to combat Darkseid.

Justice League (Vol. 2) #6 (Apr. 2012) The Justice League meets the New God from Apokolips, Darkseid.

DARK DAY

Joined by Aquaman and Cyborg, the new teammates argue among themselves over who should lead the super group, while battling incoming waves of parademons and defending themselves from the attack of overzealous American soldiers. The discussion is shelved when Darkseid from Apokolips arrives, disabling the fledgling team with one strike.

Super Seven

There is little any one Super Hero can do against the power of Darkseid. Only by working together are they able to defeat the evil entity that has come to claim humanity. Driven by Batman's cunning plan, Superman's raw power, and Wonder Woman's unparalleled bravery, the seven Super Heroes put aside their differences and, in the process, earn the trust and adoration of the people of Earth.

Justice League (Vol. 2) #6 (Apr. 2012) The new Justice League members combine their powers to defeat Darkseid.

GODS ANEW

After the reality-altering Flashpoint event, everything is changed—even the Gods. No longer representative of their past iconic selves, the new Olympians have discarded togas and the iconic images emblazoned upon them by Greek culture, and now take on forms representative of a new and modern world.

Apollo

In this reality, Apollo believes the throne of Olympus is his birthright, and wages war against Wonder Woman and his family to secure it. It is this act that provokes the First Born, and threatens to tear all realms asunder.

Hermes

Playing by no one's rules but his own, Hermes alienates most of the other Gods in his quest to protect the baby Zeke—the last son of Zeus. In the process, Hermes grants Wonder Woman the power of flight, later facing the Amazon in battle.

Athena

Absent from Olympus, Athena secretly exists within Wonder Woman's friend Zola, mother of Zeke. Later, Athena allows Zola to continue to exist, as the Goddess of Wisdom transforms herself into an owl.

Hades

An eternity watching over the suffering of souls has left Hades—who also calls himself Hell—filled with self-loathing. It takes Wonder Woman's timely intervention with a weapon of Eros to force the Lord of the Dead to accept himself.

Hephaestus

It is through Hephaestus that Wonder Woman learns much of her true origins. It is revealed that there are male Amazons. As infants, they had been traded to Hephaestus in exchange for weapons, and raised by the God to be blacksmiths.

Aphrodite

The Goddess of Love and Beauty rarely allows herself to be seen, and her apparent love of privacy extends into the realm of Olympian politics. Consequently, little is known of this incarnation of Aphrodite.

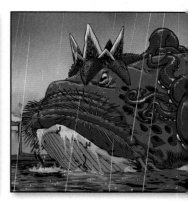

Hera

Driven to rage by Zeus' infidelity, much of Hera's time is spent wielding her wrath on Zeus' illegitimate children. Temporarily stripped of her power by Apollo, this Hera incarnation learns lessons in humility from Wonder Woman.

Artemis

The Goddess of the Hunt, Artemis is fierce and fast and ready to fight. On many occasions, she has clashed in combat with Wonder Woman while standing in support of her brother Apollo's claim to the throne of Olympus.

Poseidon

The God of the Sea's nature is now present in his form —that of an impossibly monstrous, ocean-dwelling creature. Poseidon seeks to ensure his dominion remains true, refusing to allow Zeus' children to threaten his rule of the sea.

Zeus

Zeus is Wonder Woman's father—a secret kept for a long time. Absent from the throne in a move to ensure the longevity of his rule, Zeus has been reborn as his own last-born son, Zeke—destined to succeed Zeus.

Demeter

Often quiet in the games of the Olympian Gods, Demeter allies herself with Hermes, all the while staying hidden in her own realm. It is a lush and silent garden, full of impossible plant life that is an aspect of the Goddess herself.

Ares

Though ferocious and brutal as ever, this new incarnation of War understands that his existence is one wholly intertwined with peace. As such, Ares does not revel in his nature and appears weary.

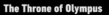

The Throne of Olympus
Olympus is a massive kingdom, extending out beyond the confines of what mortal eyes can perceive. Its design shifts, depending on who has control of the throne. During the reign of Apollo, the realm became sleek, efficient, and modern.

DATA FILE

ALIAS: War

FIRST APPEARANCE: *Wonder Woman* (Vol. 4) #4 (Feb. 2012)

OCCUPATION: God of War

AFFILIATIONS: Olympian Gods

POWERS/ABILITIES: Tremendous strength, speed, and agility, telekinetic power of weapons, shapeshifting, teleportation, control of the dead, immortality, immunity to non-magical weapons

Ares' eyes are black and empty.

Shifting Perspectives

When the world was younger, and mortal wars were fought very differently, Ares appeared quite differently. Tall, thick-muscled, with a lush red beard, Ares was every bit the warrior those of that era expected him to be. This is how he appeared when Wonder Woman first became his apprentice.

The God of War is an expert in all forms of weaponry and combat.

AN ENDLESS WAR

The God of War has grown thin and weary in this post-Flashpoint reality, the product of the never-ending conflicts that plague the mortal realm. As well as his cynical and bitter exterior, Ares remains the very essence of conflict—and is drawn to the heart of Wonder Woman's struggles.

Ares' lower legs are soaked in blood, revealing the brutal nature under his human facade.

Spirit of Destruction

The power of Ares extends far beyond his frail-looking mortal shell. For the God of War has the vast legions of fallen soldiers to call upon. They are his army, and every soldier that serves the cause of War is a hero of their own time.

> *"The purpose of war is to **end** conflict."*
>
> ARES

Of all the Olympian Gods, it seems that Ares understands the nature of his being the best. His existence is a reflection of humanity's perception of War. Where once powerful generals led in battle, now old men sit deep behind lines and command vast armies. And so the great warrior has shrunken and aged, becoming deceptively civilized in his choice of clothes. The son of Zeus and Hera is an outsider among his own kind. Ares turned to Wonder Woman when she was still young, having seen within her a kindred spirit. Ares trained the Amazon in combat and became like a father to her. However, their bond grew strained for a time when Wonder Woman refused to slay a fallen foe.

Ares wears a simple, modern suit, deceptively understating his true power and militaristic nature.

Direct Approach

Tired and weary, Ares can often be found alone, a drink in hand. But it really doesn't matter whether the God of War seeks out battle, or instead chooses the refuge of relative peace and quiet, for those around Ares will always be drawn into conflict of one form or another.

ARES: MENTOR

In the heart of conflict there is always one thing that is consistent: Ares, God of War will be found there. Unlike his predecessor in the previous universe, the post-Flashpoint Ares acts as Wonder Woman's mentor. It is a fitting role as one day, Ares' mantle will pass on to the Amazon Princess, and Wonder Woman will become the new incarnation of War on Earth.

SUPER HERO ROMANCE

In the post-Flashpoint universe, one notable difference in Wonder Woman's life is her relationship with Superman. No longer could the two powerhouse heroes be content just being friends, and their relationship turned to romance.

A PARTNERSHIP OF EQUALS

The Amazon Princess faces a difficult and very lonely road. Having reached a point in her life among mankind where she craves companionship—but under the belief that a life with a Super Hero would be too dangerous for a fragile mortal being—she succumbs to temptation and shares a kiss with Superman. This is the start of a relationship and partnership of the likes the world has never seen.

Superman/Wonder Woman Annual #2 (Dec. 2015) On top of a building in Washington, D.C., Wonder Woman and Superman open up to one another.

Justice League (Vol. 2) #12 (Oct. 2012) Wonder Woman attacks the super-villain David Graves after discovering that the captive Steve Trevor is still alive.

THE WEAKNESS OF THE HEART— EXPOSED

Having ended her relationship with Steve Trevor out of concern for his safety, Wonder Woman is horrified when a super-villain named David Graves decides that the Amazon Princess needs a tragic loss in her history—kidnapping and attempting to kill Trevor to make this point. On the verge of succumbing to guilt and despair, Wonder Woman is pulled back from the brink when she discovers that Steve Trevor has actually survived and escaped his attacker.

Superman/Wonder Woman #13 (Jan. 2015) Wonder Woman and Superman go on a date in their civilian attire.

IT'S NEVER EASY

It doesn't take long for the two to discover that their relationship will be complicated. In this reality, Wonder Woman has never had a secret identity and Superman has not dated outside of his Clark Kent persona. The lives of the two Super Heroes are so vastly different that it quickly becomes a difficult dance, determining whether the couple should openly date as themselves or in disguise.

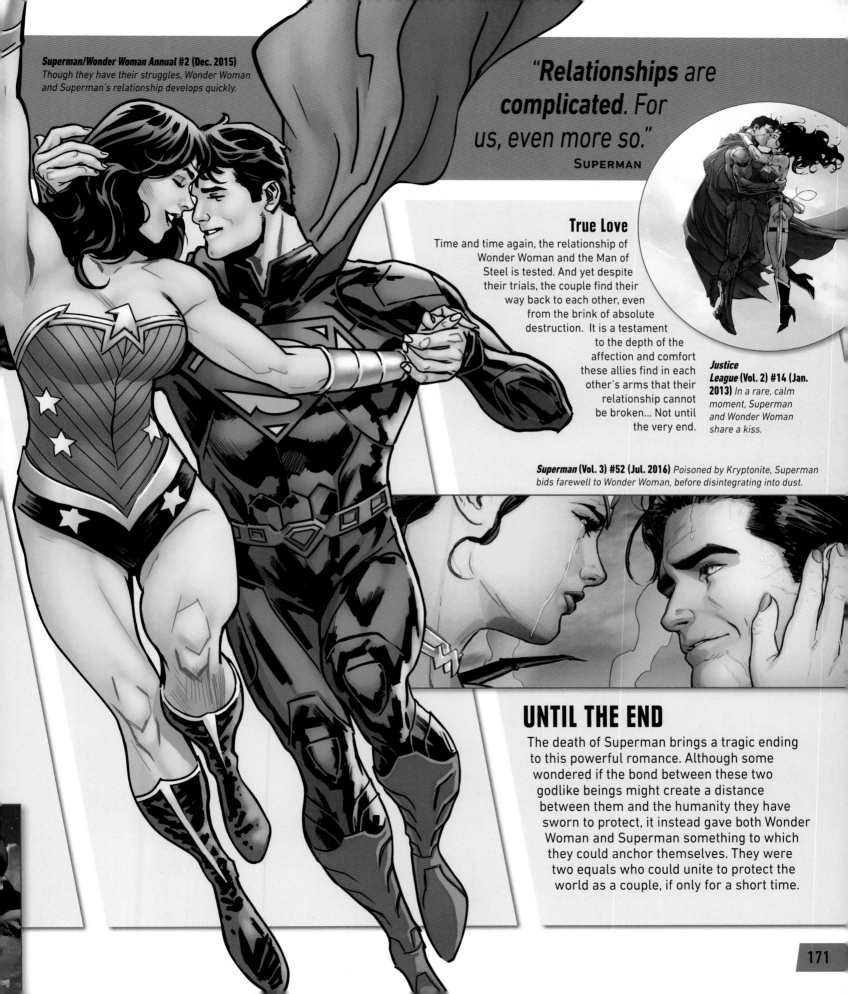

Superman/Wonder Woman Annual #2 (Dec. 2015) *Though they have their struggles, Wonder Woman and Superman's relationship develops quickly.*

> **"Relationships** are complicated. For us, even more so."
> SUPERMAN

True Love

Time and time again, the relationship of Wonder Woman and the Man of Steel is tested. And yet despite their trials, the couple find their way back to each other, even from the brink of absolute destruction. It is a testament to the depth of the affection and comfort these allies find in each other's arms that their relationship cannot be broken... Not until the very end.

Justice League **(Vol. 2) #14 (Jan. 2013)** *In a rare, calm moment, Superman and Wonder Woman share a kiss.*

Superman **(Vol. 3) #52 (Jul. 2016)** *Poisoned by Kryptonite, Superman bids farewell to Wonder Woman, before disintegrating into dust.*

UNTIL THE END

The death of Superman brings a tragic ending to this powerful romance. Although some wondered if the bond between these two godlike beings might create a distance between them and the humanity they have sworn to protect, it instead gave both Wonder Woman and Superman something to which they could anchor themselves. They were two equals who could unite to protect the world as a couple, if only for a short time.

Wonder Woman faces a foe beyond the likes of any she has ever encountered before: the deadly and brutal First Born.

Wonder Woman (Vol. 4) #21 (Jun. 2013)

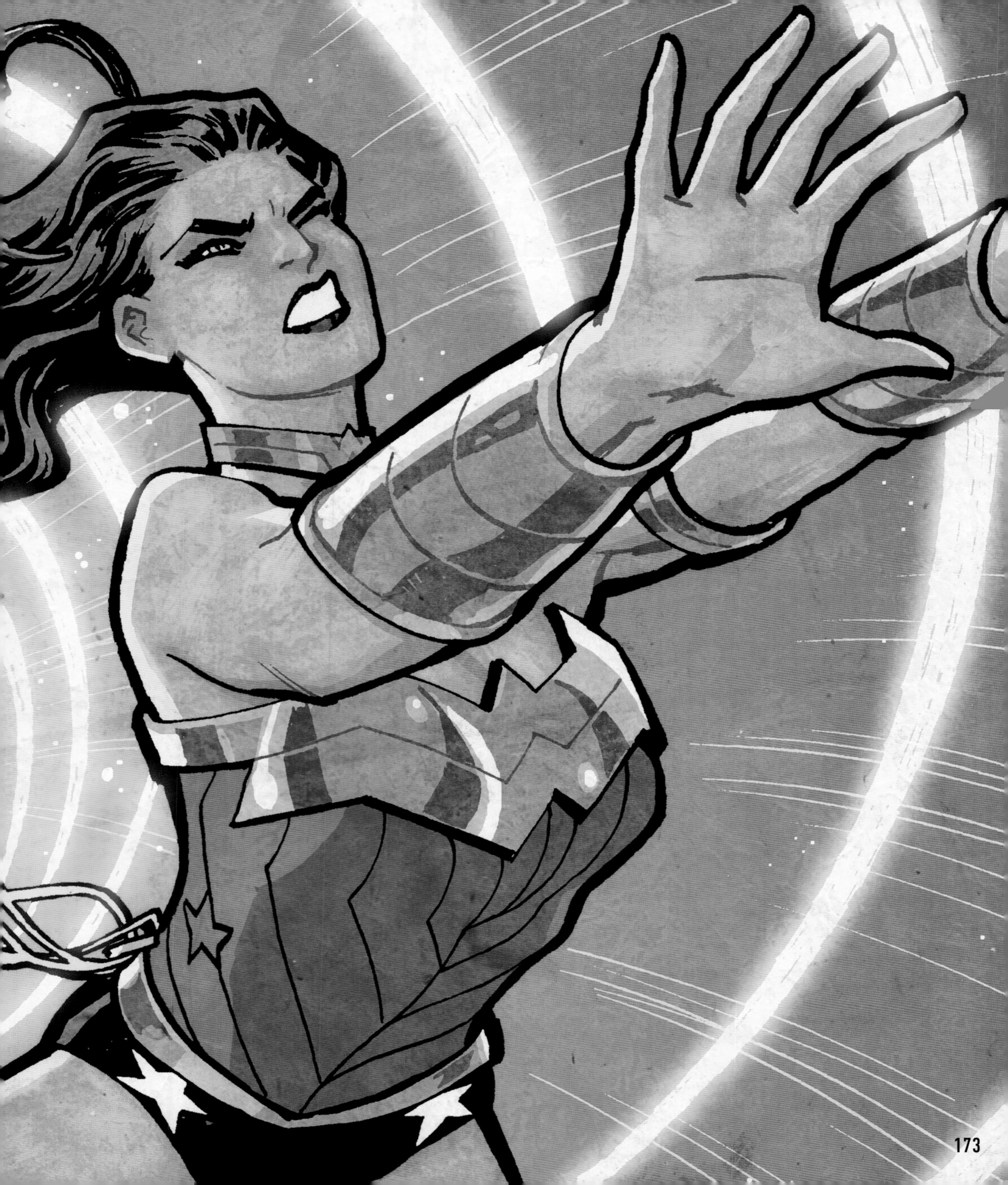

FAMILY MATTERS

Wonder Woman begins to discover that her family extends far beyond the Amazons and Themyscira. As the daughter of Zeus, she is just one of many gods and demigods, and her siblings vary in both allegiance and personality.

> "I'm anticipating... a **hell ride**. But it's one worth going on."
>
> WONDER WOMAN

MILAN

A blind, homeless demigod, Milan is Wonder Woman's half-brother and a son of Zeus. Though he cannot see by conventional means, Milan can control a vast number of flies in order to 'see' through them anywhere in the world, by the power of farsight. The overwhelming sensation has the unfortunate side effect of inflicting great pain on the demigod. Milan has formed a close friendship with Orion of New Genesis.

SIRACCA

A demigod with the power to control the wind, Siracca is Wonder Woman's half-sister. Almost a hundred years earlier, Siracca watched Hera, the wife of Zeus, tear her mother apart. Hera also tried to destroy Siracca, but due to the young girl's divine origins, she survived. Zeus later reconstituted his daughter. Wonder Woman only briefly knew her half-sister, as Siracca stayed largely out of the family affairs that would follow their meeting.

ORION

Orion is a New God who was raised on the world of New Genesis by its ruler, the benevolent Highfather. However, Orion is actually the son of the tyrannical world conqueror Darkseid, and his true birthplace is the terrible planet of Apokolips. Rejecting his origins in favor of his upbringing, Orion serves New Genesis. The New God traveled to Earth to join Wonder Woman in her fight against Zeus' estranged son, First Born, after the Highfather perceived the threat.

LENNOX SANDSMARK

Wonder Woman's half-brother, Lennox Sandsmark, was the son of Zeus and an unnamed mother. As a demigod, he had a long life span, and at the time of his first meeting with Wonder Woman, he was over 80 years old. His body was composed of a material with the same consistency as stone, which could heal from any cracks caused by injury. He died while fighting the First Born in an attempt to buy time for Wonder Woman and his half-brother Zeke, to escape First Born's rage.

ZOLA

Zola is a seemingly mortal young woman who, at the time of meeting Wonder Woman, was pregnant with a child of Zeus. Wonder Woman has devoted a great deal of time and energy to protecting Zola and her child from the wrath of the gods. In fact, Zola is more than mortal. Her body and mind are inhabited by the goddess Athena, and the child that Zola carries is not just a child of Zeus, but is actually Zeus reborn.

DESTRUCTIVE DEMIGODS

In the post-Flashpoint universe, the stakes of war between good and evil are higher than they have ever been. Wonder Woman rarely faces simple criminals, instead facing off directly against the Gods themselves.

CASSANDRA

A child of the God Zeus and a mortal woman, Cassandra once had the power to control the will of others through the sound of her voice. However, the darkness runs deep in Cassandra. After she used her vocal powers to order 40 people to kill themselves, her half-brother Lennox decided he had no choice but to remove the source of the threat—ripping out Cassandra's vocal chords. Her voice was restored with a bionic device, but her mind-control powers were lost.

DARKSEID

The true father of the New God Orion, Darkseid is the ruler of Apokolips. He is one of the few beings who belong to the realm outside time and space, known as the Fourth World. He is obsessed with discovering the Anti-Life equation—an equation that gives mathematical certainty that life is without hope—and with it, become the ultimate power of the Multiverse. Invulnerable and immortal, Darkseid rules through fear and intimidation.

A prophecy was uttered when the first born child of Zeus and Hera came into existence. Much as Chronus slew his father Uranus, and Zeus in turn slew his father Chronus, the firstborn child of Zeus was destined to seize control of Olympus from his own father. Zeus ordered his child to be destroyed—an act Hera secretly defied, sparing her infant son while abandoning him to the wild. The First Born survived for centuries, imprisoned on Earth, and was eventually forgotten. Yet all the while his rage festered and his hatred grew.

> *"I am the one with no name. The crippler of souls... **The First Born**."*
>
> FIRST BORN

The First Born's eyes have no pupils—a sign that he is a true child of the Gods.

NEW PROPHECY

In the thousands of years since the birth of the First Born, the prophecy has changed. In order to take control of the throne of Heaven, the firstborn child of Zeus must contend with the last born child of Zeus. That child is a baby named Zeke, born to Wonder Woman's young friend, Zola.

Making his Claim

After being defeated by Wonder Woman, Apollo claims the body of the First Born. The God of the Sun and current ruler of Olympus tortures and mutilates the First Born. This proves Apollo's undoing, as the First Born breaks free and claims his birthright.

DATA FILE

FIRST APPEARANCE: *Wonder Woman* (Vol. 4) #13 (Dec. 2012)

OCCUPATION: Would-be conqueror

AFFILIATIONS: Olympian Gods

POWERS/ABILITIES: Immortality, super-strength and speed, animal control, invulnerability

ALTERNATES: The First Born is a new being, having no counterparts in previous incarnations.

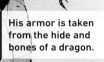

His armor is taken from the hide and bones of a dragon.

THE FIRST BORN

The dark secret of Olympus, Zeus' firstborn child wants nothing more than to ascend to the throne of the father that spurned him—wresting control of the powers of the Gods from the family he loathes.

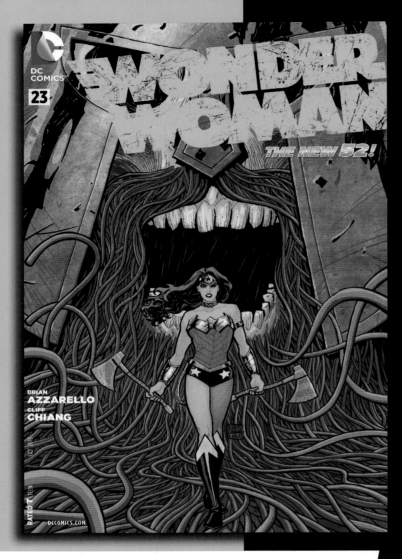

OCTOBER 2013

WONDER WOMAN
(VOLUME 4)
#23

WITNESS THE END OF WAR AND THE RISE OF THE MIGHTY WARRIOR.

The internal strife of the post-Flashpoint Greek Gods reaches its apex. The battle between the Gods and the First Born sees the final stage of Wonder Woman's decades-long transformation from agent of peace and love into the Goddess of War.

MAIN CHARACTERS:
Wonder Woman • Ares • The First Born

SUPPORTING CHARACTERS:
Orion • Zola • Zeke • Hera • Hades • The armies of War

MAIN LOCATIONS:
Westminster Abbey, UK

1 Having found themselves cornered in Westminster Abbey by vicious hordes loyal to the First Born—who claims to be Zeus' first child—Wonder Woman and her allies prepare for a final battle. In response to this threat, Ares summons those willing to fight for him: history's most honored soldiers.

2 While the battle roars around them, Orion of the planet New Genesis engages the First Born in hand-to-hand combat. It is a brutal exchange that goes poorly for the hero, ending with the mighty Orion being buried unconscious under a pile of rubble.

3 Wonder Woman removes her Bracelets of Submission and attacks the First Born. He overpowers her, and soon turns his attention toward Zeke, the infant son of Zeus. The First Born believes Zeke's death will fulfill a prophecy that a child of Zeus will kill a god to claim a throne.

4 In defense of his mother, Hera, and the infant, Ares strikes the First Born, and the two brothers soon find themselves locked in combat. Recovering, Wonder Woman reclaims her bracelets and with them her rational mind. Time is short as the First Born prepares to murder Ares and claim the mantle of War.

5 With no time left but to act, Wonder Woman drives a spear through Ares and into the First Born. As her mentor Ares falls, with his last breath he whispers of his pride for his protégée and sorrow for the burden of the mantle of War that she must now carry. The ancient prophecy is fulfilled, though not in a way anyone would have expected.

*"**Every** soldier here has a song."*

ARES

6 The First Born is defeated and Hell comes to claim the fallen God of War. It is a bittersweet victory for Wonder Woman as she joins Hades in taking Ares' body to his resting place in the land of the dead.

DONNA TROY REGENERATED

A striking reflection of Wonder Woman and sculpted from magical clay by the witch Derinoe, Donna Troy must decide her own fate: Is she a hero or a villain? In an effort to fulfill the mission for which she was created, Donna leads the Amazons to execute a newly discovered faction of males on the island. It is a bold move, and one that enrages her sister. After being touched by Diana's Golden Lasso of Truth, Donna realizes her folly.

HEALING POWERS

Having been made from magical clay, Donna Troy has the ability to heal from severe wounds. She is even capable of reattaching lost limbs—a gift she was forced to use when Wonder Woman severed both her arms in battle.

The post-Crisis Donna Troy was known to share memories and origins with all other incarnations of herself. This caused inconsistencies in her history.

*"Let us **take back** our island! Let the rivers run red with the **blood of men**."*
DONNA TROY

ORIGIN

When Queen Hippolyta died, Wonder Woman became the new leader of Themyscira. A faction of Amazons, unhappy with this leadership, used the clay remains of Hippolyta and the blood of a mortal sacrifice to craft a new being in Diana's likeness—one designed to usurp Amazon rule from the rightful princess.

DATA FILE

FIRST APPEARANCE: *Wonder Woman* (Vol. 4) #37 (Feb. 2015)

OCCUPATION: Usurper

AFFILIATIONS: Amazons

POWERS/ABILITIES: Regeneration, strength, speed, stamina

The daughter of an archaeologist and an absentee father in the form of demigod Lennox Sandsmark, Cassie was a well-traveled child—and a frustrated and angry one at that. To alleviate her angst, she turned to stealing from dig sites, museums, and artifact collectors she met through her mother. When she came into contact with a metal alien parasite, she gained access to great power—though at a terrible price.

*"I'm just a very **angry girl** looking for someone to hit."*

CASSIE SANDSMARK

Wonder Girl's lasso is actually a rope-like sliver of the alien metal armor she wears.

DISTANT RELATIVE

Despite being a granddaughter of Zeus, Cassie has no powers outside of what the alien armor grants her. She does, however, possess the fortitude and will to control the armor, even if it is difficult at times. Although Cassie is Wonder Woman's niece by blood, neither of the two heroes are aware of this relationship, and the connection between them is tenuous, at best.

DATA FILE

FIRST APPEARANCE: *Teen Titans* (Vol. 4) #1 (Nov. 2011)

OCCUPATION: Thief, Super Hero

AFFILIATIONS: Teen Titans, The Elite

POWERS/ABILITIES: Flight, strength, speed

Most of the time, the majority of Wonder Girl's armor manifests as a pair of gauntlets.

Even when not fully covering her body, Wonder Girl's armor protects her with an invisible force field.

CASSIE SANDSMARK REGENERATED

Cassandra Sandsmark dislikes the nickname Wonder Girl when she first hears it. A rebellious teen and a thief, Cassie falls into a life of super-heroics, a role she never intended for herself.

REBIRTH

After the death of Superman and the return of the original Kid Flash, Super Heroes begin to remember aspects of their history that had been forgotten. Could these memories be from a parallel universe, or are they from this universe before reality was rewritten during Flashpoint?

RETRACE YOUR STEPS

Wonder Woman returns to Olympus hoping to find answers to her questions, only to discover that the home of the Gods is not real, nor was it ever real. The First Born, Zola, Cassandra—were they all part of an elaborate lie? As her memories shift, Wonder Woman is no longer certain what to believe.

THEMYSCIRA'S CHAMPION

As the ripples of change reverberate throughout the universe, Wonder Woman revisits her place of origin. No longer a demigod, Princess Diana is awarded great powers by the Olympian Gods to aid her in the struggles she will face as Themyscira's envoy of peace.

TOGETHER AGAIN

Donna Troy is also affected by different memories. Though she was supposedly only created months earlier as part of a plot to dethrone Wonder Woman, Donna now remembers her time with the Teen Titans. She joins her former teammates to try to discover the truth of who she really is.

ENCOUNTER WITH CHEETAH

Even the Cheetah is no longer quite what she was. Now a human tainted by the dark god Urzkartaga, Barbara Minerva's origins are shifting back to something similar to her pre-Flashpoint existence. In addition, Cheetah's personality has become more savage and animalistic than ever before.

UNKNOWN FUTURE

In every corner of the universe, things are changing. Heroes and villains are remembering. But what this means for Wonder Woman and her future is still unknown. There are no more rules moving forward. It is a universe reborn. Everything is new, and anything is possible once again.

A veteran of many missions, Steve Trevor puts practicality above regulation when it comes to grooming.

Trevor is an expert in most forms of modern weaponry, and is highly experienced in handling various firearms.

DATA FILE

FIRST APPEARANCE: *Justice League* (Vol. 2) #3 (Jan. 2012)

OCCUPATION: Soldier, Government agent

AFFILIATIONS: Team 7, A.R.G.U.S. (Advanced Research Group Uniting Superhumans), Justice League of America

POWERS/ABILITIES: Exceptionally skilled pilot and hand-to-hand combatant

ALTERNATES: In a pocket universe created during an event called Convergence, Steve Trevor became a vampire.

STEVE TREVOR

Although the post-Flashpoint Steve Trevor is a soldier first and foremost, his long-standing love for Wonder Woman threatens to outshine his sense of duty. Since the romance between them ended, the man who is renowned for introducing the world to the Amazon princess, finds himself in a difficult position as they continue to work together.

AWKWARD

Shortly after Wonder Woman arrived in America from her island home, she became romantically involved with Steve Trevor. This ended after Wonder Woman saw how dangerous a life with her could be for a mortal. So Steve found himself in the difficult position of performing his duty as the appointed Justice League liaison, as well as dealing with the forced proximity of his ex-girlfriend.

ORIGIN

Post-Flashpoint, Steve Trevor returned to the role he had once held in Wonder Woman's life. A young military man who crashed on Themyscira, the badly injured soldier was returned to health. His arrival, along with other signs, was interpreted by the Amazons as a message from the Gods. Consequently, Steve witnessed a contest held to decide who would accompany him to America on behalf of the Amazons.

*"I thought you **weren't** like everyone else."*
STEVE TREVOR

Little has been revealed about Etta Candy's origins post-Flashpoint. In the immediate wake of the reality-altering event, Etta Candy served as Steve Trevor's secretary. Since then, after Kid Flash returned from the Speed Force, Etta's history has transformed. She has become Steve Trevor's superior—a commanding officer who helps introduce the world to Wonder Woman.

*"I'll try to make this **quick** then."*

ETTA CANDY

ETTA CANDY

Firm yet compassionate, Commander Candy is one of the few friends Wonder Woman has made outside of her role as a Super Hero. Though military protocol has sometimes forced the two women to stand on opposing sides of a problem, their hearts are both in the same place.

DATA FILE

FIRST APPEARANCE: *Justice League* (Vol. 2) #7 (May 2012)

OCCUPATION: Military commander, former secretary

AFFILIATIONS: A.R.G.U.S. (Advanced Research Group Uniting Superhumans)

ALTERNATES: Post-Flashpoint, Etta was younger than her Rebirth version.

Etta's non-nonsense attitude is mirrored in her determined expression.

In her office-based role as commander, Etta wears a smart suit.

SUPPORT

After working alongside both Steve Trevor and Wonder Woman for more than a decade, Etta has come to accept that where one goes, the other will inevitably follow. This is true even during the long break-ups between Wonder Woman and Steve. It is a difficult and painful time for Etta to watch both her friends struggling with their relationship.

ORIGIN

It is believed that Urzkartaga was once a benevolent god who developed a voracious taste for sacrificial blood. At some point in his history, women became his jailers, their power confining him to the limited mystical jungle he has inhabited for so long. Beyond that, his nature, including his origins, is unknown to all.

Power Hungry

Urzkartaga has accrued many allies by using his limited powers to influence mortal beings. Some are like Andres Cadulo, mortal men hungry for the power of oppression that the plant God represents. Through these soldiers, Urzkartaga terrorizes villages and captures people to sacrifice.

> "My bride, **remember** your vows..."
>
> **URZKARTAGA**

URZKARTAGA

Urzkartaga is known to take many forms, inhabiting plants and corrupting their shape to suit his needs. In truth, his essence is limitless, but bound by ancient magic. Hungry for blood, the plant God seeks sacrifices in order to gain the one thing he needs to escape his prison—a body of flesh.

Urzkartaga's body is a shell composed of living plant matter.

FALLEN GOD

There are many worshippers of Urzkartaga scattered across the globe—an indication of how vast the plant God's reach once was. And though many whisper the God's name, Urzkartaga's will is limited to a jungle of mystical origins, shrouded in mist. Everything within this realm is tainted and twisted, reshaped to reflect the sinister consciousness of Urzkartaga.

DATA FILE

FIRST APPEARANCE: *Wonder Woman* (Vol. 2) #29 (Apr. 1989)

OCCUPATION: God

AFFILIATIONS: Unknown

POWERS/ABILITIES: Plant manipulation, possession, divine empowerment

ALTERNATES: In a previous reality, the only physical representation of Urzkartaga was a harmless, inanimate, potted plant.

Dangerous Liaison

It is rumored that Urzkartaga is a jealous god, and that he curses those who would be his bride if they have ever loved another male entity. This is what he told Cheetah when he enslaved her, though much of what the plant God told his supposed bride has been revealed to be lies and manipulation.

Cult of the Vine

Using his essence to corrupt, the plant God transforms those that come to him willingly into the Bouda—animal-human hybrid beings that are overwhelmed with the same blood lust as Urzkartaga. The most valued of his servants is his bride—one who consumes the sacrifice with him and gains great power and a terrible thirst for death. His bride is currently the power-hungry Cheetah.

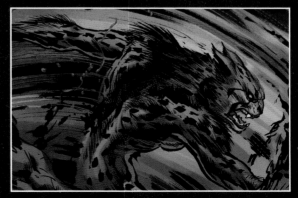

Urzkartaga's body can regrow and heal almost instantly from any physical wound.

LIES OF A GOD

Searching for answers to the shifts in her memory, and unable to find her way back to Themyscira, Wonder Woman seeks the help of an old friend and vicious enemy—Barbara Minerva, also known as Cheetah. The former foe agrees on one condition—that the Amazon helps her face her terrifying husband, the plant God Urzkartaga.

THE ENEMY OF MY ENEMY

By seeming coincidence, Wonder Woman has tracked down Cheetah in the same jungle. The Amazon seeks the help of Cheetah in locating the lost island of Themyscira. The villain agrees to help if Wonder Woman will destroy the plant God known as Urzkartaga. By doing so, she will free Barbara Minerva from Cheetah's curse.

WELCOME TO THE JUNGLE

Under the command of Etta Candy, Steve Trevor and his men embark on a mission to the Okarango region of Bwunda, in an effort to take down the self-styled warlord Andres Cadulo. Cadulo is a mass murderer known for kidnapping young girls from local villages. In an attempt to cut off Cadulo's men, Steve and his soldiers encounter an unnatural jungle.

Wonder Woman (Vol. 5) #3 (Sep. 2016) *On a mission to find the missing girls, Steve leads his men into the strange jungle.*

Wonder Woman (Vol. 5) #3 (Sep. 2016) *Wonder Woman implores her former friend, Cheetah, to help her.*

> ## *"Free me from my **currrse**."*
> CHEETAH

Wonder Woman (Vol. 5) #7 (Nov. 2016) *Wonder Woman puts up a fight against the plant God.*

INTERNAL STRUGGLE

Cadulo summons the plant God, but before he can merge with its being, Wonder Woman and her unlikely ally arrive to stop the ceremony. Cheetah subdues Cadulo, while Wonder Woman battles Urzkartaga. Outmatched by the sheer power of the god, Wonder Woman calls to Cheetah for assistance, but Urzkartaga does the same.

FREE

Wonder Woman comes to the realization that the plant God has one weakness—women. The kidnapped girls were meant to become brainwashed into serving him. But when Cheetah tells the young girls that the plant God intends to sacrifice them, they encircle the being with Wonder Woman's Golden Lasso of Truth. The spell is broken, and the plant God is banished—freeing Minerva from the curse of Cheetah.

Wonder Woman (Vol. 5) #5 (Oct. 2016) *Cadulo prepares to sacrifice Steve Trevor in order to transform himself into Urzkartaga's avatar.*

SOLDIER IN DISTRESS

Steve finds the missing girls, but he and his men are captured by Cadulo, who turns out to be serving Urzkartaga. The warlord believes that through human sacrifice, he will become the new avatar of the plant God, and lead an army to conquer the world. While Cadulo prepares Steve for sacrifice, Wonder Woman and Cheetah fight their way into Cadulo's hideout.

Wonder Woman (Vol. 5) #7 (Nov. 2016) *With Urzkartaga defeated, Barbara returns to her human form.*

INFINITE POSSIBILITIES

The many incarnations of Wonder Woman's character prove that the Multiverse allows for infinite possibilities. A few of the more unique iterations of the amazing Amazon show just how varied and strange the alternate realities of the Multiverse can be.

EARTH-11

This Earth is the home of Wonderous Man, champion of the Amazons. Here, the Amazons never went into seclusion. Instead they shared their technology and culture with the entire world, inspiring many generations of women to become leaders and heroes.

EARTH-30

Allied with the Communist government of Russia and an ally of a Russian version of Superman, this Wonder Woman is forced to break her Golden Lasso of Truth. In so doing she saves her ally, but at a high price.

EARTH-C-MINUS

This rabbit version of Wonder Woman (Wonder Wabbit) fights alongside Super Squirrel, the Batmouse, and Aquaduck, among other heroes. The JLA—Just'a Lotta Animals—battles the villains that continually threaten this amusing and absurd universe.

EARTH-23

Nubia of Themyscira mirrors a known Amazon of the pre-Crisis reality, a long-lost sister of Diana. In this reality, Nubia is Wonder Woman of Amazonia, and is devoted to her mission to bring liberty and equality for all.

EARTH-34

Princess Diana of Amazonia is kidnapped by an evil incarnation of Steve Trevor, and forced to marry him. She escapes and becomes Wonder Woman—fighting for freedom in a misogynistic city ruled by Jack the Ripper.

EARTH-18

The Wonder Woman of this reality fights alongside the Justice Riders. A superpowered sheriff of the small town known as Paradise, Diana Prince fights the railroad baron Maxwell Lord, and a professor named Felix Faust.

EARTH-59

An identical version of Wonder Woman, Princess Tara Terruna exists on a duplicate Earth where she rules her kingdom. In her quest for peace, Princess Tara struggles against the oppressive Duke Dazam.

"AND NOW WE TURN TO ANOTHER BLANK PAGE.
A FUTURE STANDING BEFORE US LIKE A FRESHLY-FALLEN SNOW.
AWAITING THAT FIRST MARK, THAT FIRST FORWARD FOOTSTEP.

A NEW JOURNEY TO BE STARTED.
A NEW PROMISE TO BE FULFILLED.
A NEW PAGE TO BE WRITTEN.

GO FORTH UNTO THIS WAITING WORLD
WITH PEN IN HAND, ALL YOU YOUNG SCRIBES,
THE OPEN BOOK AWAITS.

BE CREATIVE.
BE ADVENTUROUS.
BE ORIGINAL.
AND ABOVE ALL ELSE, BE YOUNG.

FOR YOUTH IS YOUR GREATEST WEAPON, YOUR GREATEST TOOL.
USE IT WISELY."

WONDER WOMAN #62

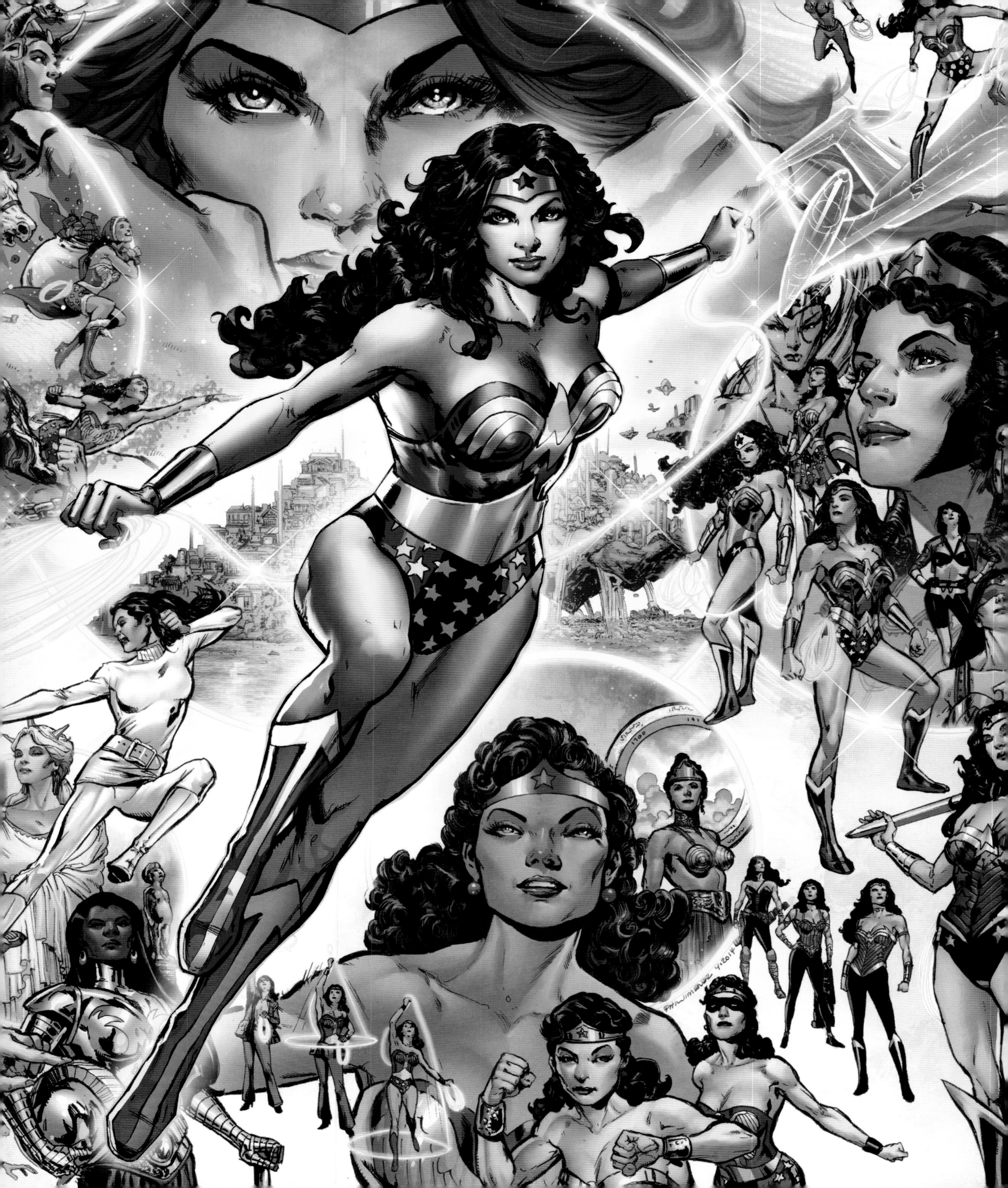

INDEX

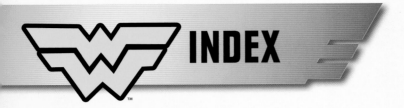

I

J

K

L

M

N

O

P

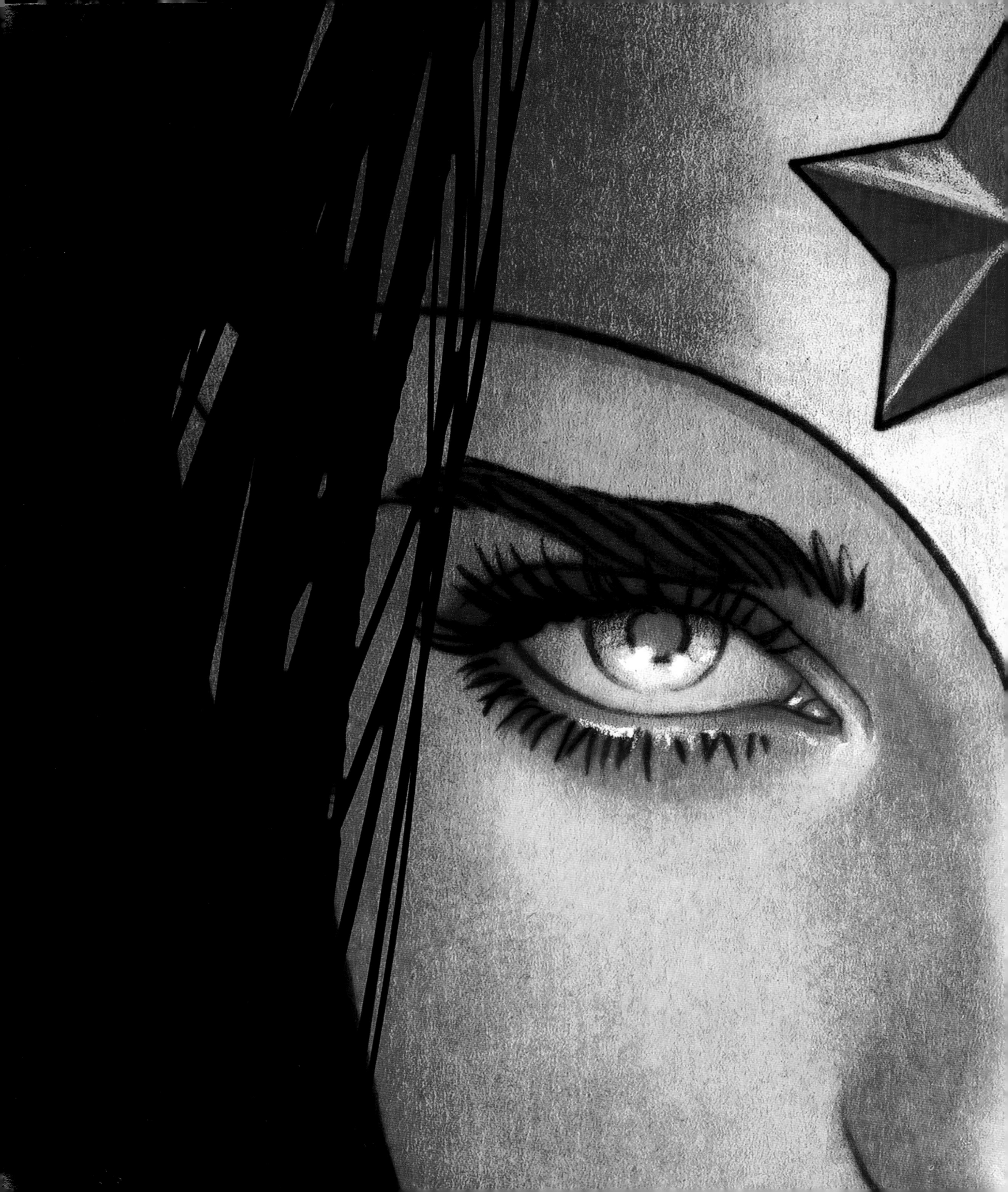

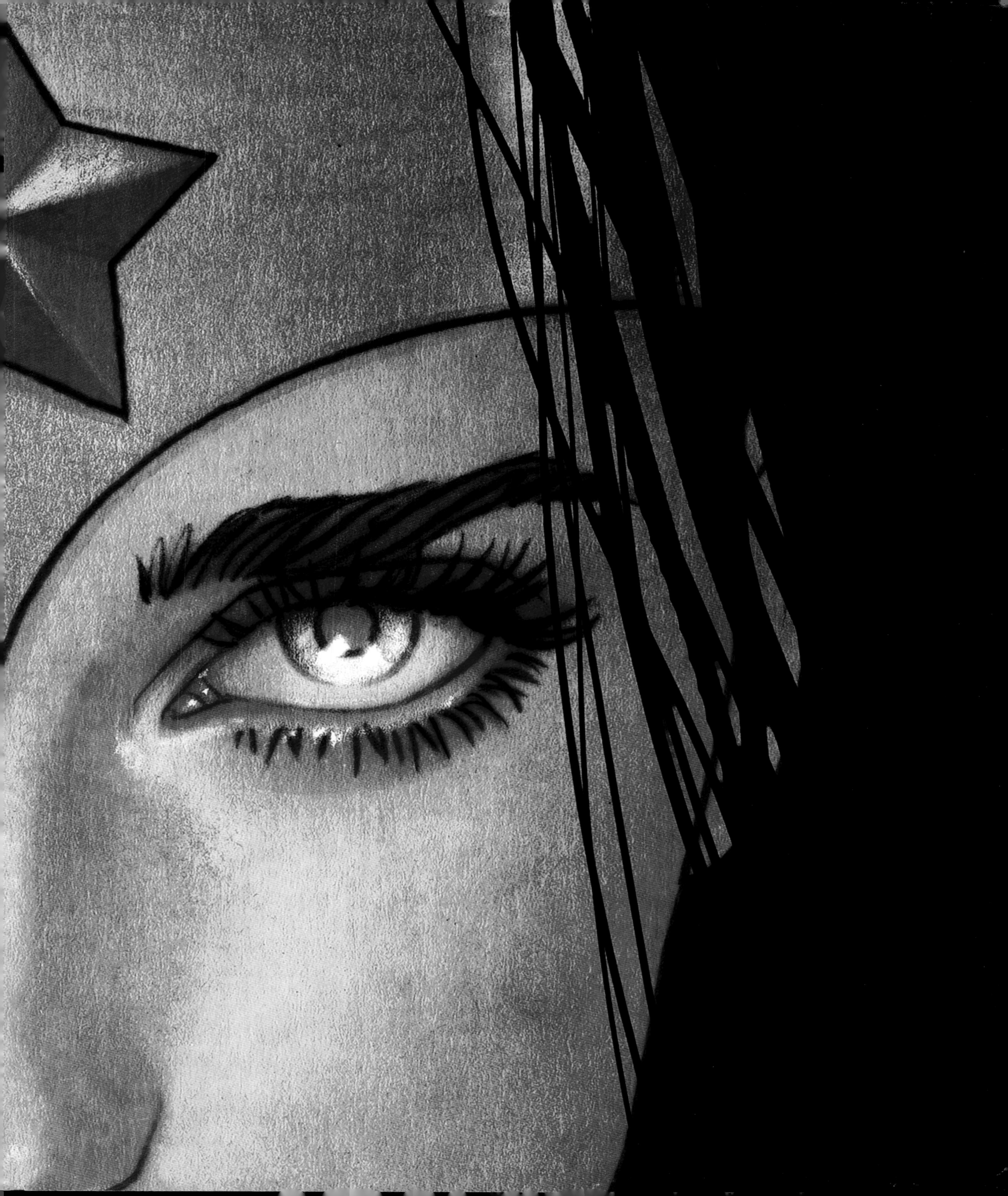

ACKNOWLEDGMENTS

The Publisher would like to thank: Leah Tuttle, Joe Daley, Hank Manfra, Jim Hancock, Erin Vanover, Doug Prinzivalli, John Wells, Josh Anderson, and Amy Weingartner; Ruth Amos, Natalie Edwards, and Lauren Nesworthy for editorial assistance; Vanessa Bird for indexing and proofreading; and Alex Evangeli for picture research.

LANDRY Q. WALKER: All my thanks on this book go my amazing friend Liz Marsham, my patient editors, and my wife who listened to me talk about Wonder Woman for months and months on end.

ARTISTS/INKERS/COLORISTS: Neal Adams, Mike Allred, Brad Anderson, Murphy Anderson, Ross Andru, Stan Aschmier, Tony Atkins, Shawn Atkinson, José Avilés, Bernard Baily, Darryl Banks, Matt Banning, David Beaty, Ed Benes, BIT, Alex Bleyaert, Brian Bolland, Brett Booth, Geraldo Borjes, Ron Boyd, Pat Broderick, John Byrne, Nick Cardy, Bernard Chang, Cliff Chiang, Scott Clark, Matthew Clarke, Iban Coello, Gene Colan, Vince Coletta, Kevin Conrad, Darwyn Cooke, Andrew Currie, Tony S. Daniel, Jose Delbo, Jesse Delperdang, Mike Deodato Junior, Tom Derenick, Johnny Desjardins, Jean Diaz, Dick Dillin, Ed Dobrotka, Rachel Dodson, Terry Dodson, Derec Donovan, Bob Downs, Mike Esposito, David Finch, Creig Flessel, Richard Friend, Jenny Frison, Sandu Florea, Joe Gallagher, Alex Garner, Alé Garza, Dick Giordano, Johnathan Glapion, Al Gordon, Wade Von Grawbadger, Mick Gray, Dan Green, Tom Grummett, Ig Guara, Yvel Guichet, Ron Harris, Frank Harry, Don Heck, Daniel Henriques, Gilbert Hernandez, Hi-Fi Design, Bryan Hitch, Sandra Hope, Richard Horle, Tanya Horle, Adam Hughs, Dave Hunt, Carmine Infantino, Mikel Janín, Alex Jay, Georges Jeanty, Phil Jimenez, Dave Johnson, J.G. Jones, Ruy José, Justiniano, Gil Kane, Karl Kerschl, Karl Kesel, Jack Kirby, Andy Kubert, Harry Lampert, Andy Lanning, Carol Lay, Jim Lee, Steve Leialoha, John Livesay, Aaron Lopestri, David Lopez, Julian Lopez, Emanuela Lupacchino, Kevin Maguire, Doug Mahnke, Mike Manley, Pablo Marcos, Laura Martin, Marta Martinez, Roy Allan Martinez, Aaron McClellan, Tom McCraw and Wildstorm FX, Lena Medina, Jesús Merino, Lee Moder, Sheldon Moldoff, Jim Mooney, Trevor Moore, Rags Morales, Tomeu Morey, Carlos Mota, Patricia Mulvihill, Brian Murray, Todd Nauck, Martin Naydel, Martin Nodell, Graham Nolan, Irv Novick, Dennis O'Neil, Jerry Ordway, Agustin Padilla, Pascal, Yanick Paquette, Andre Parks, Sean Parsons, Bruce D. Patterson, George Pérez, Harry G. Peter, Joe Phillips, Howard Porter, Joe Prado, Bruno Premiani, James Raiz, Norm Rapmund, Ivan Reis, Cliff Richards, Andrew C. Robinson, Alex Ross, Joe Rubinstein, Matt Ryan, Bernard Sachs, Jesús Saíz, Javier Saltares, Marco Santucci, Nicola Scott, Trevor Scott, Bart Sears, Stephen Segovia, Mike Sekowsky, Miguel Sepulveda, Jerry Serpe, Liam Sharpe, Scott Shaw, Howard Sherman, John Sikela, R.B. Silva, Joe Simon, James Sinclair, Cam Smith, Paul Smith, Dietrich Smith, Ray Snyder, Dave Stewart, Lary Stucker, Goran Sudzuka, Curt Swan, Ty Templeton, Art Thibert, Matthew Wilson, Phil Winslade, Matt Wagner, J.H. Williams III, Harold Wilson Sharp, Tatjana Wood, Mike Zeck.

The publishers have made every effort to identify and acknowledge the artists whose work appears in this encyclopedia.